A Student's Guide to Research and Writing

Making Sense

Education

MARGOT NORTHEY
JON G. BRADLEY

OXFORD
UNIVERSITY PRESS

OXFORD
UNIVERSITY PRESS

Oxford University Press is a department of the University of Oxford.
It furthers the University's objective of excellence in research, scholarship,
and education by publishing worldwide. Oxford is a registered trade mark of
Oxford University Press in the UK and in certain other countries.

Published in Canada by
Oxford University Press
8 Sampson Mews, Suite 204,
Don Mills, Ontario M3C 0H5 Canada

www.oupcanada.com

Library and Archives Canada Cataloguing in Publication

Northey, Margot, 1940–
Making sense in education : a student's guide to research
and writing / Margot Northey & Jon G. Bradley.

(Making sense series)
Includes index.
ISBN 978–0–19–544372–1

1. Education—Authorship—Handbooks, manuals, etc.
2. Academic writing—Handbooks, manuals, etc.   I. Bradley,
Jon   II. Title.   III. Series: Making sense series

LB1033.5.N67 2012   808.06'637   C2012-904389-3

Cover images: Microscope © Mara Radeva/iStockphoto,
Paintbrushes © Kemal Bas/iStockphoto, Blue Lockers © Carmen Martínez
Banús/iStockphoto, Basketball and Shoes © Pascal Genest/iStockphoto

Oxford University Press is committed to our environment.
This book is printed on Forest Stewardship Council® certified paper
and comes from responsible sources.

Printed and bound in Canada

1 2 3 4 — 16 15 14 13

CONTENTS

PREFACE

The *Making Sense* series would not be complete without a specific volume aimed at elementary and secondary school teachers. The classroom practitioner communicates to students and parents on a very practical and factual level. Information concerning individual academic progress must be conveyed clearly so that everyone understands the current situation and possible outcomes.

Beginning teachers enter a world in which the written word reigns supreme. Teachers write constantly, from hasty notes and assignment notations to workshop summaries and report card comments. Depending on the situation, this writing can be playful or serious, but it must always be grammatically correct.

This book focuses on the unique writing world and point of view of the teacher. It not only reinforces standard notions of professional writing but also explores many other facets of the everyday writing life of teachers, including summaries, critiques, education portfolios, formal letters, and e-mails. Technology is an important part of this life; therefore, a marginal icon indicates passages that discuss how technology can enhance such writing tasks.

ACKNOWLEDGEMENTS

This book would not have been possible without the support of my wife, Barbara. Finally growing tired of my constant complaining about the lack of an introductory writing book for teacher candidates, she challenged me to compile such a volume.

I must also thank those many colleagues who were part of the vibrant Writing Centre of the Faculty of Education at McGill University. Specifically, thank you to Patrick Dias for having the wisdom to conceive of such a unique place to pursue all forms of professional writing and to Anthony Paré for allowing me to be a part of that exceptional collection of interesting people.

Along with the publisher, I would like to acknowledge the anonymous reviewer and the following reviewers, whose thoughtful comments and suggestions helped to shape this text: Yvette Daniel, University of Windsor; Allan MacKinnon, Simon Fraser University; Olive Ridler, Nipissing University; Robert Smilanich, University of Alberta; Larry Swartz, University of Toronto;

LeRoy Whitehead, Queen's University; Robert Whiteley, University of British Columbia, Okanagan; and Meguido Zola, Simon Fraser University.

Additionally, my heartfelt thanks to those at Oxford University Press who toiled to make this book much better than originally envisioned, specifically acquisitions editor Stephen Kotowych, developmental editor Tamara Capar, and copy editor Janna Green.

Last but by no means least, I offer my thanks to those countless students in the Faculty of Education at McGill University who endured my many and varied attempts to capture their imaginations and make writing a meaningful and fun endeavour.

Jon G. Bradley
Montreal, Quebec

A NOTE TO THE STUDENT

In your new role as a teacher, you will be surrounded by and often immersed in the world of writing. Regardless of the level or subject matter you teach, you will always be—at heart—a language instructor. You and your students must be able to express concrete notions in as clear a manner as possible. One way to achieve this fluidity is via the written word.

Writing is not easy. In some ways, writing is almost a Herculean task in that it is a slow process that appears to be bound by all manner of regulations. However, practice does make perfect; the more you write and engage in the writing process, the better you will become. As you become a more proficient writer, you will also take more linguistic risks and ultimately become a more reflective person.

In some cases, your writing will be very formal (a research essay or a conference presentation) and at other times a bit more intimate (a handwritten note on a project or a letter to a parent). You will use the entire medium at your disposal and engage writing through such means as handwritten comments and letters, SMART Board exercises, and typed comments on report cards. In a sense, you will be engaged in the older forms of writing while you also explore the limits of the digital possibilities. This reality is both challenging and exciting.

Whatever your method or experience, you are always the example. Your words and ideas must set standards and be a model that others can emulate. Therefore, you must steel yourself to meet high standards, master spelling oddities and grammatical quirks, and strive for clear sentences and paragraphs.

A NOTE TO THE INSTRUCTOR

Some of your students will dread the writing process. English is not the easiest language to write, and it has its share of linguistic and stylistic issues. The contrast between British and American spelling, along with the intrusion of technological shorthand, presents the writing instructor with challenges. Further, those whose first language is not English may bring their own challenges to the class.

While it is clear that elements of modern technology, such as spell check and endnote functions, have made some of the details of writing easier, there is no question that the heart and soul of the process—the exploration of ideas—still demands careful thought and development. To date, technology has not yet mastered the art of creativity.

This book discusses many forms of writing so that the beginning teacher may see writing through a variety of lenses. In some cases, your students will be quite familiar with a specific lens; in others, a new realm will be explored.

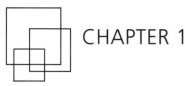

CHAPTER 1

Writing in Education

OBJECTIVES

- To utilize pre-planning as an organizational strategy
- To target writing with a clear purpose and for a specific audience
- To develop a wide variety of guidelines to enhance clear writing

INTRODUCTION

You are not likely to produce clear writing unless you have first done some clear thinking and careful pre-planning, and this ethereal process cannot be hurried. It follows that the most important step you can take is to leave yourself enough time to think. Psychologists have shown that you can't always solve a difficult problem by "putting your mind to it"—by determined reasoning. Sometimes when you're stuck it's best to take a break, sleep on it, and let the subconscious or creative part of your brain take over for a while. Very often a period of relaxation will produce a new approach or solution. Just remember that leaving time for creative reflection isn't the same thing as sitting around listening to music until inspiration strikes out of the blue.

INITIAL STRATEGIES

Writing is about choosing what ideas you want to present and how you want to present them. Practice makes decision-making easier, but you will still have to choose with each piece of writing, no matter how fluent you become.

You can narrow the field from the start if you realize that you are not writing for just anybody, anywhere, or any particular reason. With any writing you do, it's always a sound strategy to ask yourself basic questions:

- What is the purpose of this piece of writing?
- Who is the reader/audience?

Your first reaction may be, "Well, I'm writing for my instructor to satisfy a course requirement," but that's not specific enough. To be useful, your answers have to be more precise and targeted.

Think about the Purpose

Depending on the assignment, your purpose in writing an essay may be any one (or more) of the following:

- to show your knowledge of a specific topic or designated text
- to show that you understand certain educational terms or theories
- to show that you can do independent research
- to show that you can apply a specific curriculum theory to new material
- to show your ability to evaluate primary and/or secondary sources
- to show that you can think critically and/or creatively

An assignment designed to see if you have read and understood specific material requires a different approach from one that's meant to test your critical thinking. In the first case, your approach will tend to be *expository*, with the emphasis on presenting facts. In the second case, you will probably want to structure your essay around a particular argument or assertion that other people might dispute. Your aim in this kind of *argumentative*, or *persuasive*, essay is to bring your reader around to your point of view.

Think about the Reader/Audience

Thinking about the reader does *not* mean playing up to the instructor. To convince a particular person that your own views are sound, you have to consider his or her way of thinking. If you were writing a paper on the benefits of single-parent families for a sociology professor, your analysis would be different than if you were writing for an economics or history professor. You would have to make specific decisions about the terms you must explain, the background information you need to supply, and the details you offer to convince that particular reader.

In the same way, if you plan to write a paper defending tax credits for families paying private-school tuition (and your reader is a big supporter of public education) or a paper arguing that students with special needs should not be integrated into the regular stream (and your reader has a child with special needs who is integrated), you will have to anticipate any arguments that the reader may raise so that you can address them. If you don't know who will be reading your paper—professor, tutorial leader, or marker—just imagine someone intelligent, knowledgeable, and interested, someone skeptical enough to question your ideas but flexible enough to adopt them if your evidence is convincing.

Think about the Length

Before you start writing, you will also need to think about the length of your assignment in relation to the time you can spend on it. Specifically, how many words/pages are needed to either fit the assignment protocols or meet your own demands? If both the topic and the length are prescribed, it should be fairly easy for you to assess the level of detail required and the amount of research you will need to do. If only the length is prescribed, that restriction will help you decide how broad or how narrow a topic you should choose. You should also keep in mind how much the assignment is worth. A paper that is worth 50 per cent of your final grade will merit more of your time and effort than one that is worth only 10 per cent.

Think about the Tone

In everyday writing to friends you probably adopt a casual tone, but academic and professional writing is always more formal. Just how formal you need to be will depend on the kind of assignment and the instructions. In some cases—for example, if your psychology professor asks you to describe certain personal experiences in a journal—you may be able to use an informal style. Essays and reports, however, usually require a more formal tone. Likewise, letters to parents, comments on report cards, and memos to administrators demand clarity of thought and execution. What kind of style is too informal for most academic work? Here are the main signs:

USE OF SLANG

Notwithstanding the use of slang and various verbal expressions in spoken English and accepting that the occasional slang word or phrase may, with great care, be useful for special effect, frequent use of slang and slang expressions is not acceptable in academic or professional writing. In fact, most slang and accompanying expressions are either regionally specific and/or short-lived. They may mean different things to different groups at different times. (It was not too long ago that the term *gay* simply meant "happy"; additionally, think of how widely the meanings of *hot* and *cool* can vary, depending on the circumstances.) In a formal essay, where clarity of expression is important, it's always better to use words with well-established meanings that will be understood by the greatest number of readers.

Never use common text-messaging or Twitter expressions (for example, *BRB*: "be right back") in academic or professional writing. While these three- or four-letter "words" may be appropriate among friends, they are not suitable for professional writing.

EXCESSIVE USE OF FIRST-PERSON PRONOUNS

Since a formal essay is not a personal outpouring, you want to keep it from becoming *I*-centred. There is no need to begin every sentence with "I think" or "In my view" when the facts or arguments speak for themselves. It's certainly acceptable to use the occasional first-person pronoun if the assignment calls for your point of view, as long as your opinions are backed by evidence. Also, if the choice is between using *I* and creating a tangle of passive constructions (for example, "It is hoped that it can reasonably be concluded, based on the evidence that has been presented, that . . ."), it's almost always better to choose *I*. (A hint: when you do use *I*, it will be less noticeable if you place it in the middle of the sentence rather than at the beginning.) In specific letters and notes to parents and students, *I* can safely be used and, in fact, must be used when describing educational situations of a first-hand basis. Here are some examples of ways to avoid both *I*-centred and unnecessarily passive sentences:

✗   Having analyzed the new curriculum, I believe it is flawed.

✗   The new curriculum, having been analyzed, appears to me to be flawed.

✓   When analyzed, the new curriculum seems flawed.

✗   In this essay, Edward Thorndike's portrayal of the classroom environment will be investigated, and the repeated conflict between individual actions and collective efforts will be discussed.

✓   [better] In this essay, I will investigate Edward Thorndike's portrayal of the classroom environment and discuss the repeated conflict between individual and group actions.

✓ [best] This essay will investigate Edward Thorndike's portrayal of student actions and discuss the repeated conflict between individual and group situations.

FREQUENT USE OF CONTRACTIONS

Generally speaking, contractions such as *can't* and *isn't* are not suitable for academic or professional writing, although they may be fine for personal letters, in-house memos, or other informal kinds of writing—for example, this handbook. This is not to say that you should avoid using contractions altogether; even the most serious academic writing can sound stilted or unnatural without any contractions. Just be sure that, when you use contractions in an essay, you use them very sparingly; excessive use of contractions makes formal and professional writing sound chatty, informal, and less serious.

Finding a suitable tone for academic writing can be a challenge. The problem with trying to avoid excessive informality is that you may be tempted to go to the other extreme. If your writing sounds stiff or pompous, you may be using too many inflated phrases, long words, or passive constructions. When in doubt, remember that a more formal style is the best option.

Think about Presentation

Any written project must be neat and of the highest visual quality. If appropriate, place formal essays and term papers in binders. In a similar vein, letters and memos must be presented on quality bond paper and be visually appealing. Just as you would not go out on a date with a stain on your shirt, every piece of writing that you present must be void of rips, tears, or smudges.

GUIDELINES FOR WRITING

Whenever you embark on a writing project, try to keep the following guidelines in mind:

- Think about your audience.
- Be clear about your subject and your purpose.
- Define your terms in plain English, depending on the audience.
- Include only relevant material; don't pad your writing to achieve a certain number of words.
- Strive for consistency of expression throughout the work.
- Make sure that your statements, analysis and presentation of data, and documentation of sources are accurate.
- Order your information logically and use subheadings if appropriate.

- Be simple and clear in expressing your ideas. This means not only avoiding unnecessary technical and foreign terms but also using active verbs so as to avoid the overuse of the passive verb *to be*.
- Make sure that your argument is coherent.
- Draw conclusions that are clearly based on your evidence. Be very careful not to interject a personal opinion not supported by facts.
- Allow yourself as much time as necessary to work on drafts before completing the final copy.
- Make sure to edit and proofread your work carefully; if possible, have a friend edit your work.

In the chapters that follow we will consider some of these guidelines in greater detail.

USING BIAS-FREE LANGUAGE

As concern with political correctness has grown, it has become more important than ever to avoid bias in the language we use—both spoken and written. Just as you give thought to your reader(s) and to the kind of tone you wish to create, you will also want to take pains to use language that steers clear of any suggestion of bias, no matter how unintentional it may be.

The potential for bias is far-reaching, involving gender, race, culture, age, disability, occupation, religion, and socio-economic status. Although our society hasn't come up with ideal solutions in every case, developing an awareness of sensitive issues will help you to avoid using biased language.

Gender
At one time, it was acceptable to refer to a person of either sex as *he*, a practice still preferred by some traditionalists:

If an educational helper becomes redundant, he will receive a severance package.

But as sensitivity to sexist language has increased, we have become more careful about this use of a generic pronoun. Here are some options for avoiding the problem:

- Use the passive voice:

A severance package will be given to any educational helper who becomes redundant.

- Restructure the sentence:

  An educational helper who becomes redundant will receive a severance package.

- Use he or she (or he/she), although this phrase is very cumbersome and should be used sparingly:

  If an educational helper becomes redundant, he or she will receive a severance package.

- Use the plural form:

  If educational helpers become redundant, they will receive severance packages.

Another potential trouble spot involves gender-specific nouns, such as *stewardess*, *waitress*, or *fireman*. The solution in these cases is to look for gender-free words, for example, *flight attendant*, *server*, or *firefighter*.

Race and Culture

The names used to describe someone's racial or cultural identity often carry negative connotations for some readers. For example, consider the term *Negro*. The search for neutral language has produced alternatives such as *black* or *African Canadian*. We have similar problems with the term *Indian*, with alternatives such as *Aboriginal*, *Native*, *Indigenous*, *Inuit*, *First Peoples*, and *First Nations*. The best approach is to find out what the racial or cultural group in question prefers. Even if there isn't an easy answer, being aware of a potential problem is already part of the solution.

Always be aware of why you need to identify the race or culture. If such identification does not impact the centrality of your work, do not use the term. On the other hand, a person's ethnicity and/or gender may be germane to the issues at hand. In these latter cases, care and sensitivity must be displayed.

There are many other areas where the effort to develop and use neutral language has made an impact. To be politically correct, writers usually refer to citizens over a certain age as *seniors* rather than *old people* and to someone as *challenged*, having *special needs*, or even being *delayed* rather than being *handicapped*. Occasionally the search for neutral language leads to ever-changing terms or vague euphemisms, such as when *garbage collector* became *waste collector*, then *sanitation engineer* or *sanitation specialist*. Whatever the situation, be sensitive to the power of the words you use and take the time to search for language that is as bias-free as possible but not cumbersome.

As you read articles, books, and other curriculum materials from previous decades, you will come across words and expressions that are now deemed unacceptable. However, if you decide to use a direct quotation to illustrate a point in your writing, you must quote the sentences exactly. You are not permitted to alter past words and expressions to meet an evolving cultural standard that did not exist when the original work was written.

SOME FINAL COMMENTS

Prospective teachers must be aware of the power of the terms applied to students and how these words and expressions may be viewed and interpreted. For example, "Sam is delayed in reading" may not mean the same as "Sam cannot read at level two." Equally important is the underlying message conveyed to Sam and his parents.

Teachers and other educational professionals have a habit of using specific terms and abbreviations. While these may be of some particular use and interest to those within the field, such words are often confusing to other people. Therefore, choose proper nouns, technical words, and unusual expressions with care. Be sure to offer clear explanations and qualify commonplace words if used specifically within the educational landscape.

CHAPTER 2

Writing an Essay

INTRODUCTION

Research clearly shows that writing improves with practice. One way to practise is to schedule a regular time for writing. For example, you could set aside 30 minutes every day to work on a writing assignment, summarize lecture notes, or formulate outlines and thesis statements. When writing academic essays, following a few simple steps in planning and organizing will also lead to better results. This is not a one-size-fits-all process, and the amount of time you spend on each stage will depend on the nature of the assignment. For a short, straightforward essay requiring little research, you will likely spend most of the time drafting and editing. For a more complex essay, when you must include secondary sources and references, over half of your time will likely be spent on research and planning. Understanding the total process of completing a written assignment will serve you well, whether you are a first-year undergraduate, a graduate student, or a beginning teacher.

THE PLANNING STAGE

Some students claim that they can write essays without any planning at all. On the rare occasions when they succeed, their writing is usually not as sophisticated as they might think. More often, students who try to write a lengthy essay without planning just become frustrated. They get stuck in the middle and don't know how to finish or become befuddled with references. In some cases, the relief from simply handing in the project provides a short-lived euphoria that hides poor planning, sloppy organization, and weak thought.

In contrast, most experienced writers maintain that the planning stage is the most important part of the whole process. Certainly, the evidence shows that poor planning most often leads to disorganized writing. In the majority of students' essays, the single greatest improvement would not be better research or even better grammar but better organization.

This insistence on planning doesn't rule out exploratory writing. Many people find that the act of writing itself is the best way to generate ideas or to overcome writer's block; the hard decisions about organization come after they've put something down on the page. Whether you organize before or after you begin to write, you need to plan at some point.

In *Problem-Solving Strategies for Writing in College and Community*, Linda Flower (1998) summarizes the use of plans in the writing process. Plans are important, but they must not become a stagnant driving force closed to change and refinement. Therefore, bear these points from Flower in mind:

1. Every plan can be altered, changed, and, if need be, scrapped.
2. Even a flawed plan is better than no plan at all.
3. Plans are instructions to you and need not be shown to others.
4. There is no such thing as a standard or formal plan model; any structure that makes sense to you is valid.
5. Once a writing project is completed, the plan is thrown away and never used again.

Read Primary Material

Primary material is the direct evidence—usually books, articles, or personal interviews—on which you will base your essay. Surprising as it may seem, the best way to begin working with this material is to skim it. Don't just start reading from cover to cover. Look at the table of contents first, scan the index, and even read the preface and/or introduction to get a sense of the author's overall purpose and general plan. Acquiring an overview of the material will allow you to focus your questions for a more purposeful and analytic second reading. An important caveat: this initial read is done without any note-taking or underlining. Read for impact—pay attention to what jumps out, salient points, major arguments, etc.

Make no mistake: a superficial reading is not all you need. You still have to work through the material carefully a second time (and maybe even more as you complete the assignment). However, an initial targeted skim—followed by a focused second reading—will give you a much more thorough understanding than one slow reading focused on every word and thought.

Always be sure that you have a firm grasp of the primary material before you turn to secondary sources (analyses, comments, or reviews of the primary material). Instructors in some disciplines discourage secondary reading in introductory courses. They know that students who turn to commentaries may be so overwhelmed by the weight of authority that they will rely too heavily on them.

In other instances, students are encouraged to review recent literature on their topics to see where their views stand in relation to those of the experts. However, if you turn to commentaries as a way around the difficulty of understanding the primary source or if you base your argument solely on the interpretations of others, you may produce a trite or second-hand essay that does not meet the standard for adequate research and development. Your interpretation could even be incorrect because, at this stage, you might not know enough about a subject to be able to evaluate the commentary. Secondary sources are an important part of learning and are essential to many research papers, but they can never replace your own active and careful reading of the primary material.

Analyze Your Subject

Whether the subject you start with is one that has been assigned or suggested by your instructor or is one that you have chosen, it is bound to be too broad for an essay topic. You will have to analyze your subject in order to find a way of limiting or focusing it into more manageable parts.

ASK QUESTIONS

The best way to analyze is to ask questions that will lead to useful answers. How do you form that kind of question? Journalists approach their stories through a six-question formula: *who? what? where? when? why?* and *how?* For example, *what* questions regarding a novel taught in secondary school might include "What contrasts of character are there?"; "What role do the minor characters play?"; "What are the good or evil qualities of the characters?" *Why* and *how* questions are often the most productive because they take you beyond information gathering and force you to analyze and interpret. For example, "How does the author portray women (or old age or Aboriginal people)?"

To take another subject, consider some of the questions you could ask about merit pay for teachers:

- *What* are the economic costs associated with merit payments? *Where* would this money come from?
- *Who* will benefit from a merit-pay program and *who* may be disadvantaged?
- *Who* decides on merit pay and *what* procedures will be implemented to allocate the merit?
- *What* appeal procedures will be in place?
- *How* will the overall program be evaluated?

Most often, the questions you ask initially—and the answers to them—will be general, but they will stimulate more specific questions that will help you refine your topic and develop a thesis statement. Additionally, asking probing questions may identify "dead ends" and save much time and effort in the writing stage.

TRY THE THREE-C APPROACH

A more systematic scheme for analyzing a subject is the three-C approach. This technique forces you to look at a subject from three different but inter-connected perspectives by asking basic questions about *components*, *change*, and *context*:

Components:
- What parts or categories can the subject be broken down into?
- Can the main divisions be subdivided?

Change:
- What features have changed?
- Is there a trend?
- What caused the change?
- What are the results of the change?

Context:
- What is the larger issue surrounding the subject?
- In what tradition or school of thought does the subject belong?
- How is the subject similar to and different from related subjects?

What are the *Components* of the Subject?

In other words, how might the subject be broken down into smaller elements? This question forces you to take a detailed look at the subject and helps you to avoid oversimplification and/or easy generalization.

Suppose that your assignment is to discuss Saskatchewan's education policies. After asking yourself about components, you might decide that you can split the subject into (1) provincial policies and (2) national policies. Alternatively, you might divide it into (1) economic policies, (2) political policies, and (3) social policies. Because these components are still too broad, you might break them down further, splitting economic policies into (a) fiscal and (b) monetary policies; separating political policies into (a) relations with local districts and (b) relations with other international groups, such as the United Nations; and even subdividing social policies according to newly identified immigrant groups.

Similarly, if you were analyzing the impact of changing the traditional school year into a 12-month cycle, you might ask, "Who might be opposed to such a scheme?" "Who is in favour?"

What Features of the Subject Suggest *Change*?

This question helps you to think about trends. It can also point to antecedents or causes of an occurrence, as well as to the likely results or implications of a change.

On the subject of the 12-month school schedule, you might further investigate other school districts that have attempted this change and compare school drop-out rates before and after its implementation. You could also look at the anticipated impact on summer programs and possible complications to family vacation plans.

Suppose you have decided to focus on your local school district's cyberbullying policies. You might consider whether those policies shifted over a period of years. Did schools express contradictory views in different situations? What caused changes in a specific policy? What role did parents and the media play in the evolving policies? What tragic incident focused opinion and galvanized action? Did the regulations from another school district or other political body impact your local decision-making processes? What were the effects of these changes?

What is the *Context* of the Subject?

To what particular philosophy or tradition does the subject belong? What are the similarities and differences between this subject and related ones? The following are typical context questions:

- How do the current educational policies compare with those of previous administrations? How do they compare with the policies of related provincial and local governments?
- How do students who attend a 10-month system and those who attend a 12-month system differ in terms of provincial examination results?
- How has the rate or nature of cyberbullying changed as a result of the new policies? How does cyberbullying in your area compare to neighbouring systems?

General as most of these questions are, you will find that they stimulate more targeted questions and thoughts about the material from which you can choose your topic and decide on your controlling idea. Remember, the ability to ask intelligent questions is one of the most important, though often under-rated, skills that you can develop for any work, in university, college, or other educational settings.

Analyze a Prescribed Topic

Even if the topic of your essay is supplied by your instructor, you still need to analyze it carefully. Underline key words and terms to make sure that you don't neglect any important elements. Distinguish the main focus from subordinate concerns. A common error in dealing with prescribed topics is to emphasize one portion while giving short shrift to another. Give each part its proper due, and make sure that you actually do what the instructions tell you to do.

One very common essay-writing error is to misread the question and/ or to go off on a tangent that is outside the assignment's frame of reference. Consider the instructions implicit in these verbs, which often appear in pre-scribed topics:

outline   State the major elements of the material simply, without much development of each point (unless asked).

trace   Review by looking back on stages or steps in a process or on causes of an occurrence. Find the starting point and note changes over time.

explain   Show how or why something happens without expressing your opinion.

discuss   Examine or analyze in an orderly way. This instruction allows you considerable freedom, as long as you take into

account contrary evidence or ideas. Be careful not to
highlight a single issue or become fixated on a specific
point of view. Personal experiences are sometimes
appropriate, but they must not make up the bulk of the
response.

compare   Examine similarities and differences in a balanced manner.

evaluate   Analyze strengths and weaknesses, as well as provide an
overall assessment. This high-level task can call for a
personal opinion based on the data and/or life experiences.

Develop a Thesis

Not all essays centre on arguments. Yet every essay, even the expository kind,
needs a controlling idea around which all the material can be organized. This
central idea is usually known as a thesis, thesis statement, or thesis idea (though
you may prefer to think of it as a theme in the case of an expository essay).

If you have decided to present an argument, you will most probably want
to create a *working thesis* as your focal point. This statement doesn't have to be
final—bear in mind Linda Flower's (1998) strategy about changing your plan
at any stage. Your working thesis simply serves as a linchpin, an overarching
idea holding together your information and ideas as you organize. It will help
you clearly define your intentions, make your research far more selective and
relevant, and focus your essay.

At some point in the writing process, you will probably want to make
your working thesis into an explicit thesis statement that can appear in your
introduction or early on in your essay. You may choose to put your thesis
statement later in the paper or just generally imply it; however, a strong and
focused thesis statement near the beginning of a paper lets the reader clearly
know what's about to happen and helps guide and locate your arguments.

A RESTRICTED THESIS

A restricted thesis is one that is narrow enough for you to examine thoroughly
in the space you have available. Suppose, for example, that your general
subject is classroom management. Such a subject is much too broad to be
handled properly in an essay of a thousand words; therefore, you must restrict
it in some way and create a line of argument for which you can supply adequate supporting evidence.

Following the analytic questioning process, you might find that you
want to restrict your topic by time: "Classroom management strategies have
evolved from external teacher control to internal student control." Or you

may attempt to limit it by age: "Classroom management strategies for young students must emphasize physical safety." Also, you may contrast cultural notions within society by asking, "How might classroom management strategies fit the cultural and religious lifestyles of newly arrived immigrants?"

As another example, if you were to examine some of John Dewey's theories in relation to curriculum development, you might restrict your reading to *The School and the Child* (1906) and *Schools of To-morrow* (1915). In this way, you could concentrate on two specific volumes and delve more deeply into their ideas.

A UNIFIED THESIS

A unified thesis must have one main controlling idea and must not be burdened with a variety of compounding notions. In some ways, this format appears to be one of the easiest to follow. However, a common error is to inadvertently turn a unified thesis into a non-unified one.

"The school board trustees introduced new policies to combat cyberbullying at the elementary grade levels" is a clear and focused unified thesis. But "The school board trustees introduced new policies to combat cyberbullying at the elementary grade levels, but all members lost in the following elections because they had not dealt with the secondary school issues" complicates the thesis by introducing factors that mitigate the original point. What is the unified thesis here: the introduction of cyberbullying at the elementary levels or reasons for losing the following election? Remember, a unified thesis is a powerful statement that shows clear direction and intent.

A PRECISE THESIS

A precise thesis must not contain vague terms such as *interesting* or *significant*, as in "Ms. Beverley Wong, the first principal of the local school, was an interesting educational administrator." What does this statement actually mean, "effective or daring in the implementation of educational policies," "controversial," or "intriguing"?

Such words are usually subjective. More importantly, they add nothing of substance to the discussion and in no way clarify the subject. Therefore, don't say, "John Dewey uses difficult words in his writing." Such a statement assumes that everyone finds his words difficult (which may not be the case) and contributes nothing to any serious debate. It might be more interesting to state, "John Dewey constantly attempted to find new words to describe evolving educational scenes." In the latter sentence, the use of contextualized language is placed in a much more inviting realm.

Remember to be as specific as possible when creating a thesis in order to focus your essay. Don't just make an assertion—give the main reason for it.

Research Your Topic

If your topic requires more facts or evidence than the primary material provides or if you want to know other people's opinions on the subject, you will need to carry out appropriate research. Some students like to read about the subject before they decide on an essay topic; for them, the thesis statement comes after the exploration. You may find this approach useful for some essays, but it's generally better to narrow your scope and plan a tentative thesis before you turn to secondary sources—you'll save time and produce a more original essay.

EXPLORE LIBRARY RESOURCES

The importance of getting to know your way around a library can't be stressed enough. You don't want to be so overwhelmed by its size and complexity that you either scrimp on required research or waste time and energy trying to find information. Remember, most academic libraries have orientation seminars specifically designed to show you where and how to find what you want. Take advantage of these services. Librarians will also be glad to show you the relevant bibliographies, indices, online databases, and other reference tools. Once you are familiar with these basic sources, you will be able to check for available material systematically.

In addition to on-site resources, libraries offer a wealth of online services that are accessible from remote locations. Instead of making a trip to the library, you may be able to conduct your research from your home computer. For example, online catalogues provide remote access to a list of all the holdings at your library, including books, videos, instructional materials, children's and young adult literature, microforms, and print journals. A simple electronic search will give you a list of relevant sources in your library and, as most university libraries are linked to a wider library network, other materials. In some cases, interlibrary loan services enable quick access to many off-campus resources, often at little or no cost.

Electronic databases simplify your search for information because they make millions of journal articles available from a single source. University libraries subscribe to numerous online services that index a subset of smaller databases, thereby acting as gateways to a huge network of online journals. A single search gives you access to articles in hundreds of different journals. Some of these articles will be available in full text, allowing you to read them online, as well as save, print, or e-mail them.

It is important to follow the specific security and management protocol of your library. While many wide-ranging searches and article retrievals can be conducted from an off-campus location, each library has its own requirements. There are also sometimes restrictions depending on program, database request, and student status.

SEARCH THE WEB

 In addition to the online services provided by your library, you may wish to access the huge volume of information available on the Internet. No doubt you already have favourite search engines and are accustomed to finding information on just about anything. The billions of sites accessed by your search engine will produce a wealth of information almost instantly. Be careful, though. You will want to invest significant time and energy in making sure that the information you locate is reliable and accurate.

Evaluating Online Sources

Unlike academic journals, which are peer reviewed and tend to be reliable sources of information, many websites do not have editorial boards and publish material that has not undergone any kind of peer review. Anyone can publish online, as the current proliferation of blogs confirms. Be sure that the author or publisher of the material you use has the necessary authority to lend credibility to his or her work. When using information from the Web, always apply this litmus test: if in doubt, don't use it.

 Here are some tips for evaluating websites:

- **Pay attention to domain names.** In June 2008, the Internet Corporation for Assigned Names and Numbers (ICANN) made sweeping changes to the way top-level domains (TLDs) are assigned. The following will provide you with a guideline in assessing the nature of a site and how reliable it might be.

    .ca (Canada): This is an example of a country code TLD; other examples include .uk (United Kingdom), .de (Germany), and .eu (European Union). A .ca domain can be bought by any corporation or resident satisfying the Canadian Presence Requirement. These sites may be useful, but can be authored by a wide range of companies or individuals, so be alert for a particular perspective.

    .com (commercial): These domains are the most popular and can be bought by any individual or company, usually for the purpose of doing business online. However, publishers such as Oxford University Press have a *.com* address and host academic journals with the stated goal of bringing high-quality research to a wide audience. Other examples are online encyclopedias, dictionaries, newsletters, newspapers, and magazines. These organizations, as well as having a commercial purpose, have the intention of disseminating sound information. Don't discard any *.com* site out of hand, but do investigate it thoroughly.

.edu (education): This domain is used almost exclusively by educational institutions in the United States. Educational domains used in other countries include *.ac.uk* (United Kingdom) and *.edu.mx* (Mexico). Canadian universities typically use the *.ca* domain.

.gc.ca (Government of Canada): This domain is privately held by the Canadian government, with control over subdomains held by organizations and departments such as Health Canada and Environment Canada. Information on these sites should be factual, but you need to be alert for political bias. The same holds true for provincial government websites, which have no specific domain name.

.gov (government): These sites are used by government entities of the United States. As with *.gc.ca* sites, they should contain factual information but can also be selective in which facts they include, so be on the lookout for a skewed agenda.

.net (network): This domain is traditionally used by organizations involved in Internet infrastructure, but there are no formal restrictions on who may register a *.net* domain name.

.org (organization): Originally designated for not-for-profit firms and non-governmental organizations, *.org* domains can now be registered by any individual or business. Check these sites carefully to determine who publishes them and assess their potential accuracy.

There may be additional clues in the URLs of some sites. For example, a tilde (~) indicates a personal page where you are likely to find expressions of opinion.

- **Look for information about the site host.** You should be able to find a statement on the home page identifying the host, listing contact information, and giving details about the credentials of any contributors to the site.

- **Determine the currency of the site.** There should be a clear indication of when the material was written, published, and last revised.
- **Evaluate the accuracy of the information.** Be sure to check facts and figures with other sources. Data published on the site must be documented in citations or a bibliography and research methods explained. If you cannot verify the facts and figures found on a specific website with any other sources, exercise caution when using such information. The newspaper adage of requiring at least two unrelated sources for verification is an excellent rule of thumb to use when selecting web-based information.
- **Avoid wikis.** These collaborative websites allow anyone to contribute or modify content. A free encyclopedia that anyone can edit may be a quick and easy way of getting information, but it's not the kind of research on which you want to base your essay.
- **Be wary of blogs.** Although some companies have official blogs that can offer good advice about subjects ranging from school reading issues to homework policies, many are simply online diaries published by a rapidly increasing number of people expressing personal opinion and nothing more. Using such unverified material can seriously undermine your essay; therefore, these kinds of sources are to be avoided.
- **Assess the overall quality of the site.** A major clue to the reliability of the website is its level of correctness and writing standard. A website containing typos, spelling mistakes, or grammatical errors is a clear indication of unprofessional and sloppy work that has not been monitored for correctness or accuracy. A web author who doesn't pay attention to these details clearly lacks fastidious research methods, and any information on the site has to be suspect.

Make Clear Notes

Finding your research material is one thing; taking notes that are dependable and easy to use is another. With time, you will develop your own best method, but for a start you might try the somewhat standard and time-tested index-card system. Simply put, you record each new idea or piece of evidence on a separate index card. The number of cards you need will obviously depend on the range and type of research you're doing. When you've finished with your note-taking, you can then easily arrange the cards in the desired order.

Some people prefer to key notes directly into a computer. It's easy to then cut and paste the notes to arrange them in a logical order. Another common way is to enter your notes via a speech recognition program. While still rudimentary in many ways, these programs do facilitate quick notes.

Whatever method you follow, remember that exact records are essential for proper references. The following are some guidelines for taking good notes:

- For every entry, check that the bibliographic details are complete, including the name of the author, the title of the source, the place and date of publication, and the page numbers. For online sources, record the URL, date of publication, and date of access. Nothing is more frustrating than using a piece of information in an essay only to find that you aren't sure where it came from. Record the bibliographic details in the citation format you plan to use for your paper; that way, you can copy the source directly when you're preparing your list of references. (You will find detailed information about citation formats in Chapter 6.)
- Never guess at a reference, fudge page numbers, or be careless with URL characters, volume numbers, and other bibliographic information. Faulty referencing will not only annoy your instructor but will also be considered academic sloppiness and, possibly, a form of plagiarism.
- Check that quotations are copied precisely and, since you may end up using only part of the quotation, be sure to mark any page breaks.
- Include page numbers for every reference, even if you paraphrase or summarize the idea rather than copying it word for word.

Create an Outline

Individual writers differ in their need for a formal plan. Some say that they never have an outline, while others maintain that they can't write without one; most fall somewhere in between. Since organization is such a common problem, though, it's a good idea to know how to create an effective plan. Of course, the exact form it takes will depend on the pattern you use to develop your ideas—whether you are defining, classifying, or comparing, for example.

If you tend to have problems organizing your writing or if you are new to this aspect of academic writing, your outline should be formal (with appropriate subheadings) and as complete as possible. On the other hand, even if your mind is naturally logical, you may find it's not enough just to jot down a few words on a scrap of paper. For most students, a well-organized outline in point form is the most useful model. If you have used index cards to organize your research materials, these can provide a simple way to begin your outline. Rearranging the cards in different orders will give you an idea of how topics fit together before you put the outline down on paper. If you prefer to work on a computer, your word processor offers a range of outline styles.

The following is an example of an outline that might fit a descriptive essay:

THESIS: John Dewey viewed public education as a vehicle to an enlightened citizenry and a road to lifelong learning.

Introduction

I.   Dewey's views of education within society
   A. Education for democracy
      1. Citizenship education
      2. Lifelong learning
   B. Personal education anchored in past experiences
   C. Education based in ethical frameworks
      1. Place of morality
      2. Place of religion
   D. Education as personal growth
      1. Education for self
      2. Education for others

II. Dewey today

Conclusion

The following example illustrates an outline for an expository project with a more descriptive theme:

THEME: The place, role, and value of homework as a viable educational task is under review in many learning communities as emerging research appears to question some long-held percepts.

Introduction

I.   Homework has served different purposes for stakeholders.
   A. Students
      1. Elementary
      2. Secondary

     B. Parents
        1. School connections
        2. Offspring connections
     C. Teachers
        1. Contact with home
        2. Reinforcement of academic program
        3. Identification of individual weaknesses

II. Main established positive features
     A. Student growth
        1. Individual self-reliance
           a) Time scheduling
           b) Meeting deadlines
        2. Individual responsibility
        3. Use of technologies outside of school time
     B. Establishing lifelong learning skills
        1. Individual research
        2. Individual academic extensions

III. Homework's emerging restrictions
     A. Academic continuation questionable
        1. Parents doing work
        2. Teacher inability to evaluate homework properly
     B. School intrusions on home life
        1. Sibling demands and workspaces
        2. Pressure to balance other outside activities
        3. Homework's impact on identified/coded students
        4. Teacher reaction to non-homework regimes

Conclusion

The guidelines for possible outlines are simple:

- **Code your categories.** Use different sets of markings to establish the relative importance of your entries. The example here moves from Roman numerals to uppercase letters to Arabic numerals to lowercase letters, but you could use any system that makes sense to you.
- **Categorize according to importance.** Make sure that only items of equal value are put in equivalent categories. Give major points more weight than minor ones.

- **Check lines of connection.** Make sure that each main category is directly linked to the central thesis and that each subcategory is directly linked to its relevant larger category. Checking these lines of connection is the best way of preventing essay muddle.
- **Be consistent.** In arranging your points, use the same order every time. You may choose to move from the most important point to the least important or vice versa, as long as you are consistent.
- **Be logical.** In addition to checking for lines of connection and organizational consistency, make sure that the overall development of your work is logical. Does each heading/idea/discussion flow into the next, leading your reader through the material in the most logical manner?
- **Use parallel wording.** Phrasing each entry in a similar way makes it easier for your reader to follow your line of thinking. For a discussion of parallel structure, see pages 158–9.

Be prepared to change your outline at any time in the writing process. Your initial outline is not meant to put an iron clamp on your thinking but to relieve anxiety about where you're heading. A careful outline prevents frustration and dead ends—that "I'm stuck. Where do I go from here?" feeling. But since the very act of writing will usually generate new ideas, you should be ready to modify your original plan. Just remember that any new outline must have the consistency and clear connections required for a unified essay.

THE WRITING STAGE

Writing the First Draft

Rather than striving for perfection from the moment they begin to write, most writers find it easier to compose the first draft as quickly as possible and do extensive revisions later. However you begin, you must never expect the first draft to be the final copy. Skilled writers know that revising is a necessary part of the writing process and that the care taken with revisions makes the difference between a mediocre essay and a good one.

Many writers, from the award winner to the elementary pupil, have faced the dreaded writer's block at one time or another. In many ways, writer's block is not something that should be feared; rather, it is a very telling juncture in the writing journey. It is a point where you can experiment with different strategies to enhance your writing skills. Listed below are a series of writing techniques and planning strategies that will help you overcome this temporary intellectual impasse. You need not embrace every strategy but only those that resonate with you and permit you to engage in the writing task.

- **Get an early start.** You simply cannot leave major writing projects to the last minute. Last-minute efforts will almost always produce mediocre results. Contemporary university and college students and beginning teachers must use their dedicated writing periods to full capacity; therefore, produce thesis statements and outlines early on in the process for all projects and assignments. Such pre-planning will result in more grounded projects.
- **Write early and often.** Do not wait until you have apparently exhausted every possible resource. A common error of less secure writers is to assume that no writing can take place until "everything" has been researched. Writing in segments or timed stages has been proven to be an efficient and more profitable strategy.
- **Focus on subtopics.** Concentrate on smaller pieces of the outline rather than the whole essay. Doing so will keep you from feeling so overwhelmed.
- **Brainstorm.** Jotting down ideas, no matter how far-fetched and outside the box, is an excellent way to free the creative juices. No idea is too outrageous or too wild to be excluded. In fact, the only rule is to note every idea. While you will sort your ideas (and probably reject some of them) later, this technique leads to unanticipated possibilities.
- **Loop or cluster.** These visual techniques allow you to further refine your topic. In a loop exercise, you circle a key word or concept from your brainstorming session and then do a focused session on that specific word. In other words, you loop back and around the isolated concept. In a cluster exercise, you write your topic in the centre of a blank sheet of paper and draw a circle around it. Then, you write and/or draw any ideas that come to mind.
- **Freewrite.** One way out of writer's block is simply to write. That is, put pen to paper or fingers to keyboard and write. The purpose of this exercise is not so much to end up with a complete or viable piece of writing as it is to give yourself permission to write about the topic in any way that you want and without evaluation. Freewriting is also unconcerned with proper spelling or grammar.

- **Visualize.** Can you draw your topic? What might *pragmatism* look like? Can you picture *evaluation*? How would you sketch *classroom management*? Many of us see things in different ways. We are unique as individuals, special in our codes of ethics, and varied in our life experiences; hence, it may be appropriate and liberating to see if you can visualize your topic.

Developing Your Ideas Further: Some Common Patterns

The way you develop your ideas will depend on your essay topic and requirements. Most essays follow one or more of a handful of basic patterns, such as those described here. Identifying the appropriate pattern will help you focus your writing.

DEFINING

Sometimes a whole essay or professional writing exercise is an extended definition, explaining the meaning of a term that is complicated, controversial, or simply important to education, such as *cyberbullying, classroom management,* or *homework policy*. Rather than making your whole paper an extended definition, you may decide to begin by defining a key term before shifting to a different organizational pattern. In either case, make your definition exact and anchored in the context; it should be broad enough to include all the things that belong in the category but narrow enough to exclude things that don't. A good definition builds a kind of verbal fence around a word, herding together all the members and cutting off all outsiders.

For any discussion of a term that goes beyond a bare definition, you should give concrete examples. Depending on the nature of your essay, these could vary in length from one or two sentences to several paragraphs or even pages. If you are defining *classroom management*, for instance, you will probably want to discuss at some length the educational theories related to both external and internal controls.

In an extended definition, it's also useful to point out the differences between the term you're defining and any others that may be related to or confused with it. In education, we tend to use a variety of commonplace words in a specific professional landscape. For example, general words and combinations such as *reports, management, grade, group work, co-operative learning, scaffolding,* and *individual education plan* all have multiple meanings defined by context. Therefore, it is essential that you clearly define the terms you use, place them in a context that will be understood by the reader, and maintain those definitions throughout the paper.

CLASSIFYING

Classifying means dividing something into its separate parts according to a given principle of selection. The principle or criterion will vary. For example, you could classify grades according to how they are assessed (informally in school or via formalized testing), over a particular period of time (a week or a term), by the conditions (open book, laboratory assessment, or real-life examples), or by a given population or subgroup (age, race, religion, and/or gender). If you are organizing your essay by a system of classification, remember the following:

- All members of a class must be accounted for. If any are left over, you need to alter some categories or add more.
- Categories can be divided into subcategories. You should consider using subcategories if there are significant differences within a category. If, for instance, you are classifying your students' home situation according to parental occupation, you might want to create subcategories according to income level and account for both stay-at-home and unemployed parents.
- Any subcategory should contain at least two items.

EXPLAINING A PROCESS

This kind of organization shows how something works or has worked, whether it is the weather cycle, the justice system, or the local school system. You need to be systematic, to break down the process into a series of steps or stages. Although your order will vary, most often it will be chronological, in which case you should ensure that the sequence is accurate and easy to follow. Whatever the arrangement, you can generally make the process easier if you start a new paragraph for each new stage.

TRACING CAUSES OR EFFECTS

A cause-or-effect analysis is really a particular kind of process discussion, in which certain events are shown to have led to or resulted from other events. Usually, you are explaining why something happened. The main warning here is to avoid oversimplifying. If you are tracing causes, distinguish between a direct cause and a contributing cause, between what is a condition of something happening and what is merely a correlation or coincidence. For example, if you discover that most new teachers are female and most secondary school dropouts are male, you can't jump to the conclusion that new female teachers are forcing adolescent males to drop out of school. Similarly, you must be sure that the result you identify is a genuine product of the event or action and that you have the data to directly support your conclusions.

COMPARING

Students sometimes forget that comparing things means showing differences as well as similarities, even if the instructions do not say "compare and contrast." Suppose, for instance, that you were comparing negative and positive effects of a specific classroom management system on two classes. The easiest method for comparison—though not always the best—is to discuss the first subject in the comparison thoroughly and then move on to the second:

positive effects: resources used
consequences observed
student actions
teacher feedback

negative effects: resources used
consequences observed
student actions
teacher feedback

The problem with this kind of comparison is that it often reads as if it is two separate, smaller essays slapped together.

To be successful you must integrate the two subjects, first in your introduction (by putting them both in a single context) and again in your conclusion, where you should bring together the important points you have made about each. When discussing the second subject, try to refer repeatedly to your findings about the first. This method may be the wisest choice if the subjects you are comparing seem so different that it is hard to create similar categories.

If you can find similar criteria or categories for discussing both subjects, however, the comparison will be more effective if you organize it like this:

resources used: negative effects
positive effects

consequences observed: negative effects
positive effects

student actions: negative effects
positive effects

teacher feedback: negative effects

positive effects

conclusion: combination of effects

Because this kind of comparison is more tightly integrated, it is easier for the reader to see the similarities and differences between the subjects. As a result, the essay is likely to be more forceful and less likely to read as two separate parts.

OTHER PATTERNS

Along with these five formats, there are several other common essay types:

- argumentative: An attempt to convince your reader to accept your point of view.
- clinical: A neutral, non-personal report of an event in which you were a participant or an observer.
- critical: A detached, non-personal description of an event in which you did not participate.
- descriptive: The most common type of paper, one that describes a particular item(s) in as much detail as possible.
- expository: Another common professional exercise, in which you demonstrate your own knowledge of something.
- illustrative: An essay that deals with more ethereal concepts, combining words and visuals to offer cogent explanations.
- narrative: An essay based on personal and professional experiences.
- research: An essay that compares and contrasts your own ideas with those of others.

Writing Introductions

The beginning of an essay has a dual purpose: to indicate your topic and the way you intend to approach it and to whet your reader's interest in what you have to say.

THE FUNNEL APPROACH

One method of introducing a topic is to place it in a context—to supply a kind of backdrop that will put it in perspective. The idea is to step back and discuss the area into which your topic fits and then gradually lead into your specific field of discussion. In other words, in your opening paragraph, you want to explain the topic briefly and broadly and then indicate a position regarding it. One of the most effective ways to structure such an opening paragraph is the funnel approach, illustrated in Figure 2.1 (see Baker & Gamache, 1998).

A funnel has a large opening at the top and a narrow one at the bottom. In the funnel approach, so too does your opening paragraph: it starts with a general statement, narrows down to some aspects, and, finally, specifically targets a concrete aspect. A funnel opening is applicable to almost any kind of essay but is most effective in dealing with a persuasive essay.

You should try to catch your reader's interest right from the start. You know from your own reading how a dull beginning can put you off a book or an article. The fact that your instructor must read on makes no difference. If a reader has to get through 30 or 40 similar essays, it's all the more important for yours to stand out. A funnel opening can help you achieve this goal, but it isn't the only way to grab the reader's attention. The following sections describe four of the most common introductory formats.

THE QUOTATION

Beginning your essay with a quotation works especially well when it is taken from the person or work that you are discussing. Alternatively, the quotation can be from someone who has a different opinion. In this way, you have either highlighted the topic with a positive quotation or provided a bit of dissonance by offering a contrasting viewpoint.

You can also use an interesting or provocative quotation from an unrelated source or author, as long as it is relevant to your topic and not so well known that it will appear trite. A dictionary of quotations (such as *The Oxford Dictionary of Quotations*) can be helpful, allowing you to search for quotes by author, key words, or, in some cases, topic.

THE QUESTION

A rhetorical question will only annoy the reader if it's commonplace or trite or if the answer is obvious, but a thought-provoking question can make a strong opening. Therefore, always frame your question so as to show some insight as opposed to simple repetition.

For example, "Should all children attend school?" is a moot point because we have specific laws that have more or less settled the issue. However, "Should parents have the right to exempt their children from generic religious instruction?" provides a more specific question with more shading for debate.

While the question is an acceptable format, it is a tricky opening because you must find the appropriate balance between commonality and creativity. You must also ensure that you answer the question somewhere in your essay.

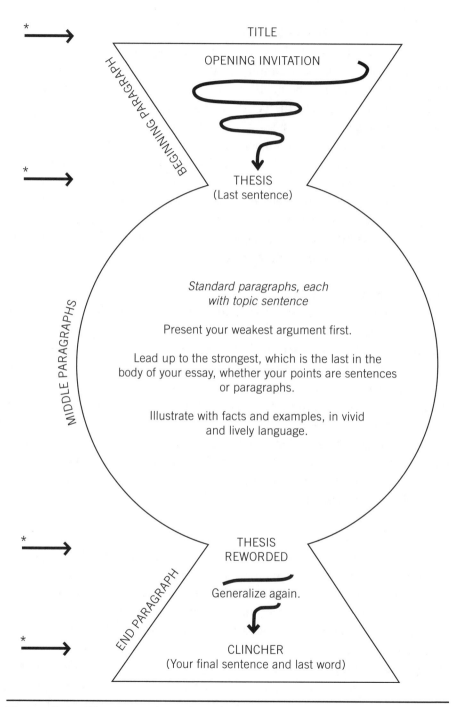

Figure 2.1 The Funnel Approach

Source: Baker, S., & Gamache, L. B. (1998). *The Canadian Practical Stylist* (4th ed.). Don Mills, Canada: Addison-Wesley, pp. 55–56.

THE ANECDOTE OR TELLING FACT

This approach is the kind of concrete lead that journalists often use to grab their readers' attention. For example, an educational sociology paper on young offenders might begin: "The bailiff leads Jimmy through a maze of corridors from the detention cell to the courtroom. A stranger to the halls of Keane County Youth Court would need a map, but Jimmy could probably find his way blindfolded; after all, he's made this trek more than a dozen times since he was 10." Save this approach for your least formal essays—and remember that the incident must really highlight the ideas you are going to discuss.

There is no question that tales can make for a powerful opening. However, unless your essay concerns a specific person or event, be sure that your anecdotes are "messaged" such that the reader will be unable to identify the people involved or other features from the sentences.

THE PERSONAL NARRATIVE

We all have varied life experiences, and an actual experience from our lives can sometimes be germane to the topic under discussion. In such a case, it may be quite advantageous to include a personal story. Such narratives add a tone of authenticity to the debate and may help to anchor what otherwise could be an intellectual analysis within a personal framework. Be careful, though, as the personal remembrance must be central to the issue and not some insignificant tangent.

For example, we have all attended schools and have had first-hand experiences with homework, classroom discipline, school examinations, and dress codes. Therefore, it may be appropriate to include a personal narrative in essays that discuss such topics.

Writing Conclusions

Endings can be painful—sometimes for the reader as much as for the writer. Too often, the feeling that one ought to say something profound and memorable produces a pretentious or affected ending. In some cases, the conclusion is nothing more than a rehash of the paper and fades in impact.

Experienced editors sometimes say that many articles and essays would be better without their final paragraphs; in other words, when you have finished saying what you have to say, the best thing to do is to stop. This advice may work for short essays, where you need to keep the central point firmly in the foreground and do not need to remind the reader of it. However, for longer pieces, where you have developed a number of ideas or a complex line of argument, you should provide a sense of closure. Readers welcome an ending that helps to tie the ideas together; they don't like to feel as though they've been left dangling. And since the final impression is often the most lasting, it's in your best interest to finish strongly. That said, simply restating your thesis or summarizing what you have already said isn't forceful enough. The following are some alternatives.

THE INVERSE FUNNEL

The simplest conclusion is one that restates the thesis in different words and then discusses its implications. Sometimes referred to as the inverse or closing funnel approach, this tactic leaves the reader with a reverse opening paragraph. That is, the writer restates the opening funnel in an opposite manner.

One danger in moving to a wider perspective is that you may try to embrace too much. When a conclusion expands too far it tends to lose focus. It's always better to discuss specific implications than to trail off into vague generalities in an attempt to sound profound.

THE NEW ANGLE

A variation of the basic closing funnel approach is to reintroduce your argument with a new twist. Suggesting some fresh angle can make your ending more compelling or provocative. Beware of introducing an entirely new idea, though, or one that's only loosely connected to your original argument. If the point is too far off-topic, it could detract from your argument instead of enhancing it.

THE FULL CIRCLE

If you began your essay by telling an anecdote, posing a rhetorical question, or citing a startling fact, you can complete the circle by referring to it again in your conclusion and relating it to some of the insights revealed in the main body of your essay. This technique provides a nice sense of closure for the reader.

THE STYLISTIC FLOURISH

Some of the most successful conclusions end on a strong stylistic note. Try varying the sentence structure: if most of your sentences are long and complex, make the last one short and punchy, or vice versa. Sometimes you can dramatize your idea with a striking phrase or colourful image. When you are writing your essay, keep your eyes open and your ears tuned for fresh ways of putting things, and save the best for the end.

THE QUOTATION FINISH

Just as you might commence a paper with an insightful quotation, so too might you close a paper with one. The potential difficulty here is that the reader may actually want you to conclude the paper in your own words so that he or she may gauge your abilities. Nonetheless, using a quotation from a recognized expert in the field can be an effective way to end a serious discussion.

THE NARRATIVE/PERSONAL ENDING

In some cases, a narrative may be an interesting manner in which to draw conclusions. Stories are powerful and pointed examples and, where appropriate, can offer an insight that might be lacking from other sources. However, be careful to use such a closing only if the topic is open to such personal observations.

Integrating Quotations

Aside from beginning or ending an essay, quotations can also be used in the main text. An embedded quotation, which can range from a short phrase to one or more paragraphs, can benefit an essay in two main ways. First, it adds depth and credibility by showing that your position or idea has the support of an authority. Second, it provides stylistic variety and interest, especially if the quotation is colourful or eloquent.

The stylistic trick to using quotations effectively is to make sure that they are properly integrated with your own discussion, that they neither dominate your ideas nor seem tacked on. To ensure that a quotation has the desired effect, always refer to the point you want the reader to take from it; don't let a quotation dangle on its own.

Generally speaking, there are three types of quotations used in academic essays:

- *Stand-alone quotations* (or *block quotations*) are usually more than one sentence and are indented and separated from the main text. Set without quotation marks and usually single-spaced, this kind of quotation enforces the text and provides authority to the writer's arguments.
- *Fully integrated quotations* are completely incorporated into the main text. Clearly set within quotation marks, these integrated quotations are effective in that they add a flow to the writer's own words.
- *Partially integrated quotations* are usually inserted at the end of a sentence and complete an idea stated by the writer. Also set within quotation marks, these quotations complete smaller ideas and can be effective when strategically placed within a body of text.

Each type has its place, and there are no rules regarding which is best or even how often one should use quotations. However, a paper must never be seen as simply a string of quotations linked together with a few words from the writer. Essays are to be original pieces in their own right, and quotations are meant to enhance and offer stylistic pauses but never overtake the writer's voice. A rule of thumb: don't quote any more than you really need. For more on quotations, see pages 64–5.

AVOIDING PLAGIARISM

Plagiarism is a form of stealing. As with other offences, ignorance is no excuse. Every university and college (and many other kinds of educational organizations) have formal policies regarding academic honesty. Everyone is required to become familiar with the information and to follow all of the dictates. Penalties for plagiarism range from a grade of zero for the specific assignment to an "F" for the course to outright expulsion from the institution. The way to avoid plagiarism is to give credit where credit is due by using the appropriate referencing style.

If you are using someone else's idea, acknowledge it, even if you have changed the wording or just summarized the main points. Don't be afraid that your work will seem weaker if you acknowledge the ideas of others. On the contrary, it will be all the more convincing; serious academic treatises are almost always built on the work of preceding scholars, with credit duly given to the earlier work.

Let's say that your Canadian history professor assigns an essay on the expulsion of the Acadians from Nova Scotia in 1755. The following is a passage from John Mack Faragher's (2005) *A Great and Noble Scheme*:

> The removal of the Acadians . . . was executed methodically by officers of the government in accordance with a carefully conceived plan many years in the making. It utilized all the available resources of the state. It included the seizure and destruction of Acadian records and registers, the arrest and isolation of community leaders, the separation of men from women and children. In the nineteenth century, operations of that kind would be directed at Indian peoples such as the Cherokees, but before 1755, nothing like it had been seen in North America. Today, the universal condemnation of ethnic cleansing by world opinion makes it difficult to defend what was done. In 2003, Queen Elizabeth II issued a Royal Proclamation acknowledging British responsibility for the decision to deport the Acadian people and regretting its "tragic consequences." (p. xix)

One student's essay includes the following passage. It is plagiarized because exact phrasing is taken from the original and no acknowledgment is given:

✗ The expulsion of the Acadians in 1755 **included the seizure and destruction of Acadian records and registers, the arrest and isolation of community leaders, the separation of men from women and children**. It was in fact the first instance of **ethnic cleansing** in North America. **In 2003, Queen Elizabeth II issued a Royal Proclamation acknowledging British responsibility for the decision to deport the Acadian people and regretting its "tragic consequences."**

To avoid a charge of plagiarism and its unpleasant and sometimes disastrous consequences, you must acknowledge your source. In the correctly documented passage below, words and phrases taken directly from the original are in quotation marks, and a parenthetical text citation is included at the end of the passage.

✓ The expulsion of the Acadians in 1755 "included the seizure and destruction of Acadian records and registers, the arrest and isolation of community leaders, the separation of men from women and children." It was in fact the first instance of "ethnic cleansing" in North America. "In 2003, Queen Elizabeth II issued a Royal Proclamation acknowledging British responsibility for the decision to deport the Acadian people and regretting its 'tragic consequences'" (Faragher, 2005, p. xix).

The following passage is also plagiarized. This student has made the common mistake of assuming that paraphrasing the information is good enough. It's not. The concept of the expulsion being an ethnic cleansing is still "borrowed":

✗ In 1755 the first instance of ethnic cleansing in North America occurred when officers of the government removed the Acadians from Nova Scotia using all the state resources at their disposal.

Remember that plagiarism involves not only using someone else's words but also expressing ideas that you acquired elsewhere without making it clear that they were taken from another source.

In the correctly documented passage below, proper acknowledgement takes the form of an in-text reference to the author with the date of the publication cited in parentheses:

✓ As historian John Mack Faragher (2005) argues in his book *A Great and Noble Scheme*, the first instance of ethnic cleansing in North America occurred in 1755, when officers of the government removed the Acadians from Nova Scotia using all the state resources at their disposal.

Where should you draw the line on acknowledgements? As a rule, you don't need to give credit for anything that's common knowledge. For example, you wouldn't include citations for lines from a national anthem or the dates of Confederation, but you must acknowledge any turn of phrase that is neither well known nor your own. And always document any fact or claim—statistical or otherwise—that is unfamiliar or open to question.

For students in a hurry (not a good state to be in), online material is a particular hazard and can cause a great deal of grief. Even though websites are instantly accessible, the material is not common property. In fact, it is the property of the individual or organization that publishes it and is protected by copyright in the same way that printed material is. It is crucial that you properly acknowledge the information that you find on a website. (The proper procedure for documenting online material is included in Chapter 6.)

THE EDITING STAGE

Often the best writer in a class is not the one who can dash off a fluent first draft but the one who is the best editor. In order to edit your work well, you need to see the completed essay as the reader will, which requires distinguishing between what you meant to say and what you have actually put on the page. For this reason, it's a good idea to leave some time between drafts so that, when you begin to edit, you will be looking at the writing afresh rather than reviewing it from memory. This is the time to go to a movie or the gym, to do something that will take your mind off your work. Without this distancing period, you can become so involved in your paper that it will be hard to see your writing objectively.

Editing doesn't mean simply checking your work for errors in grammar or spelling. It means looking at the piece as a whole to see if the ideas are well organized, well documented, and well expressed. It may mean making changes to the structure of your essay by adding some paragraphs or sentences, deleting others, and moving others around. Experienced writers may be able to check several aspects of their work at the same time, but if you are inexperienced or in doubt about your writing, it's best to look at the organization of the ideas before you tackle sentence structure, diction, style, and documentation.

Where possible, have a friend or peer edit your work (you could return the favour by editing his or her paper). Turning your ideas, thoughts, and efforts over to another for criticism can be daunting. To a certain extent, the reader is going to see into your mind. However, your work must be seen through fresh eyes. After all, you are not the most impartial reader of your own work. As you have read the same words and phrases so often, you have also come to accept their validity. An unbiased reader will catch things that you may have missed and will be able to comment on the overall thrust of the work.

If you do decide to edit your own work, the following checklist will assist you. Far from being all-inclusive, it focuses on the first step: examining the organization of your work. Since you probably won't want to check through your work separately for each question, you can group some of them together and overlook others, depending on your own strengths and weaknesses as a writer.

- Is my title concise and informative?
- Are the purpose and approach of this essay evident from the beginning?
- Are all sections of the paper relevant to the topic?
- Is the organization logical?
- Are the ideas sufficiently developed? Is there enough evidence, explanation, and illustration?
- Would an educated person who hasn't read the primary material understand everything I'm saying? Should I clarify some parts or add any explanatory material?
- In presenting my argument, do I take into account opposing arguments or evidence?
- Do my paragraph divisions make my ideas more coherent? Have I used them to keep similar ideas together and signal movement from one idea to another?
- Do any parts of the essay seem disjointed? Should I add more transitional words or logical indicators to make the sequence of ideas easier to follow?
- Do my conclusions accurately reflect my argument in the body of the work?

Another approach would be to devise your own checklist based on comments you have received on previous assignments. This method is particularly useful when you move from the overview of your paper to the close focus on sentence structure, diction, punctuation, spelling, and style. If you have a particular weak area—for example, irrelevant evidence or run-on sentences—you should give it special attention. Keeping a personal checklist will save you from repeating the same mistakes.

Your word-processing program will catch some typing and spelling errors, but it will not point out actual words that are wrongly used (such as *there* when you need *their*). You must think of any computer spell check as a useful first rather than a final check. Similarly, grammar checkers, though considerably better than when they first appeared, are still unreliable and prone to all manner of false readings. They may pick up common grammar errors and stylistic problems, but they also make mistakes and will likely never equal the judgment of a good human editor.

Also keep in mind that, for final editing, most good writers suggest working from the printed page rather than from the computer screen. Print a draft and use the hard copy for your editing and proofreading. You will read more slowly and with greater acuity, and the final product will be more polished as a result.

FORMATTING YOUR ESSAY

We've all been told not to judge a book by its cover, but the very warning suggests that we have a natural tendency to do so. Readers of essays find the same thing. A well-formatted, attractive essay creates a receptive reader and, fairly or unfairly, often gets a higher mark than a sloppy paper that is more difficult to read. While good looks won't substitute for good thinking, they will certainly enhance it.

The presentation of any kind of formal paper demands a certain degree of respectability. Individual instructors will request specific requirements, but in the absence of such demands, you should finalize your project in the following manner:

- Use margins of at least one inch (2.5 cm) to frame your text in white space. If you plan to submit your essay in hard copy in a binder, leave sufficient space in the left margin (usually two inches [5 cm]) so that interior pages can be read and turned easily.
- Use 20-pound white bond paper, letter size.

- Include a title page clearly indicating your name, paper title, and other course and identification information.
- To keep your essay as legible as possible, use only one side of the paper.
- Leave a border of approximately 1 inch (2.5 cm) on the top, right, and bottom of all textual pages.
- Use a standard 12-point font size and a legible serif script such as Times New Roman.
- Avoid the overuse of distracting visual effects such as page blocking, bolding, scripting, and coloured paper.
- Double-space the main text of your essay; use single line spacing for block quotations.
- Insert page numbers on the bottom right.
- Include a separate reference list at the end of the essay.

REFERENCES

Baker, S., & Gamache, L. B. (1998). *The Canadian practical stylist* (4th ed.). Don Mills, Canada: Addison-Wesley.

Faragher, J. M. (2005). *A great and noble scheme: The tragic story of the expulsion of the French Acadians from their American homeland.* New York, NY: W. W. Norton.

Flower, L. (1998). *Problem-solving strategies for writing in college and university.* Fort Worth, TX: Harcourt Brace.

CHAPTER 3

Writing a Professional Summary and an Academic Critique

INTRODUCTION

Throughout your career as an educator, you will summarize and evaluate works from a wide range of genres, from non-fiction to fiction, drama, research articles, and opinion pieces. As such, the professional summary and academic critique will be invaluable tools in your writing repertoire. In this chapter, we will discuss each form in relation to a particular theory: the former within transactional theory and the latter within the Rogerian method.

TRANSACTIONAL THEORY

A reader's experience with a text forms the basis of the transactional and reader-response theories of literature. These approaches were advocated by educator Louise M. Rosenblatt (1995), who was a strident proponent of people's interactive and personal relationships with literature and literary elements. In Rosenblatt's view, any literary work (including an academic paper) is a benign instrument until its words and ideas are encountered by a reader. It is in this unique and singular transaction that learning occurs:

> The special meaning, and more particular, the submerged associations that these words and images have for the individual reader will largely determine what the work communicates to him. The reader brings to the work personality traits, memories of past events, present needs and preoccupations, a particular mood of the moment, and a particular physical condition. These and many other elements in a never-to-be-duplicated combination determine his response to the particular contribution of the text. (Rosenblatt, 1995, pp. 30–31)

Let's consider a couple of examples. Have you ever reread one of your favourite books and liked it less? Why is it less appealing? Remember, the book has not changed. But you have. You have grown, had experiences, read more books, and had more conversations. The new you is reading the old book in different contexts. In Rosenblatt's view, a different transaction has occurred.

Furthermore, how many times have you and your friends read the same book only to find that you have varying interpretations? To Rosenblatt, this disagreement would be a normal and anticipated outcome. According to her, the only way to begin to solve these apparent contradictions is to return to the work itself and seek clarification directly from the literary effort.

Obviously, individuals read literature for different reasons. You may carefully read a poem to relish the rhymes, quickly read a novel to follow the plot, and slowly read an academic article to understand its argument. To Rosenblatt, efferent reading is undertaken to gain meaning and understanding, while aesthetic reading brings pleasure and experience. As a beginning educator, much of your reading will be of the efferent nature. You will engage in discussions, make presentations, and write papers to seek clarification and to solidify what corresponds with your own developing educational philosophy.

THE PROFESSIONAL SUMMARY

One form of writing that has an efferent nature is the professional summary, a neutral statement that captures the central ideas of a particular work. As the term *neutral* implies, the professional summary does not include personal comments or individual opinions but helps the reader clearly understand the main orientation of a work. Furthermore, it helps you internalize the main ideas of the piece and develop your writing skills. In many ways, the hallmarks of a well-crafted professional summary are its brevity, focus, and objectivity.

In most cases, you will write professional summaries to keep track of books and articles you have read, lectures and workshops you have attended, and even parent meetings. As with note-taking, you can keep your summaries in either paper or digital form.

Professional Summary Guidelines

We offer summaries all the time. For example, friends ask us to tell them what a movie or novel was about. However, in our daily lives, we often make the mistake of combining a summary and a critique. A clear summary will not use *I*, does not evaluate, and offers no sidebars. Unfortunately, what many of us have become used to in terms of a summary is not what is needed within educational circles. Old habits may be hard to break, but the professional summary must be recognized as a separate and legitimate form with its own guidelines:

- Be brief.
- Use your own words.
- Open with a short overview.
- Concentrate on main ideas or central issues.
- Remember the three no's.
- Do not include a conclusion.

Let's expand a bit on each of these points. As students, we are terribly concerned with page lengths and word counts. While a professional summary can be about a work of any length, the actual summary generally does not exceed 10 per cent of the original. For example, a 1,000-word article can be summarized in 100 words and a 200-page book in 20 pages or less. That said, don't get fixated on determining the length of an article or your summary. You don't need a calculator. Simply use common sense and aim, at least initially, for the 10 per cent ratio. However, this standard is just a maximum guideline. With practice, you should attempt 5 per cent.

When considering the length of the summary, think about the backs of books and DVD cases. Because space is limited, the writers attempt to capture the essence of the piece. In many cases, these summaries feature concise writing, without linking words and phrases or small details.

A professional summary must not include direct quotations of any kind. The one exception is if the author has coined a new word or phrase (such as Rosenblatt's *transaction thesis*) or used terminology in a specific way. Even if the author has explained his or her ideas in wonderful flowing prose, your role is to frame them in your own words.

Your opening paragraph must give a brief overview of the work you're summarizing. In the remainder of the summary, concentrate on the central points. Other components are to be ignored. Don't rehash the research methodology or the author's credentials and affiliations.

Bear in mind the three no's: no minor details; no repetition of points; and no personal opinions. Think of your summary as a surgical view of the piece. You are highlighting only the major points and recasting those issues in your own words without comment or embellishment.

In any professional summary, a conclusion is not needed. In a sense, the whole summary is a conclusion on its own, so you don't need to go any further.

The Two Three Process

While you will try a number of summary models and eventually choose one that fits your personality, the two three process serves as a solid starting point. In this model, there are three reading segments followed by three writing segments:

- initial read
- note read
- linking read
- first draft
- second draft
- third draft

These elements should not be combined until you become comfortable with the scheme.

Reading the work three times may sound extreme and a waste of time, but each reading uses different skills and serves a different purpose. Like skimming primary material for your essays, the initial reading is just that, a reading. Do not mark up the text or take notes. The purpose of this read is to acquire an overview of the whole piece, see how the arguments are developed, and determine the general approach.

You will use your pen or pencil in the second reading, which will be slower than the first. As you progress, you will make marginal notes and comments. However, note only those specific ideas that are of merit or worthy of reflection. In the third and final reading, confirm your notes, look for larger connections, and generally reaffirm your understanding of the piece. The third reading takes on the role of the beginning outline for the written part of the process.

Just as you're engaged in three readings, you will write three times to produce a finished product. The first draft is built directly from the last reading and involves organizing your marginal notes and comments into paragraph form. The second draft follows a rereading and editing of the first, with a concentration on the opening paragraph. At this stage, you will verify that you have not altered the author's ideas in any way by using your own words. Your third draft is a close edit for grammar, spelling, and the use of any connecting phrases.

As you internalize your own system for professional summaries, you will amass a large collection related to many aspects of your work. These summaries can be easily reviewed and added to, and they will provide a personal reference for your reading and other experiences. The ability to record such information in a precise and neutral manner will also be an asset during your career.

THE ROGERIAN METHOD

The art of oral persuasion is as old as humankind. Since we could first communicate with words, we have been attempting to convince others to do something, act in a certain way, or adopt our point of view. The ancient Greeks raised this skill to a science (known as rhetoric). As advocated by Aristotle, this model was taught in secondary schools and universities throughout the Western world for hundreds of years. Almost militaristic in its aim, the method is assertive and clearly intended to disprove an opponent's arguments. The end goal is to win; there is no compromise and no negotiation. There is also no moral or ethical component involved. The issues of right and wrong do not enter the equation, and it is quite appropriate to win an argument based on falsehoods if that is what it takes to disarm your opponent.

Based on his reaction to this method and his pioneering person-centred approach to understanding human interaction, psychologist Carl R. Rogers (1980) developed a more humanistic style that, while maintaining integrity and points of view, focused on building bridges between the speaker and audience or the writer and reader. In his view, the "I win and you lose" format characterized by the traditional Greek method was counterproductive, created lasting negative feelings, and failed to advance human empathy.

The Empathetic Position

In Rogers's approach, the writer takes on a less strident stance. Rogers argued that too many writers who followed a more classical approach to arguments actually turned off their readers by attempting to win at all costs. He felt that a more empathetic position would allow both the writer and the reader to meet over common ground and thereby be less confrontational.

As an empathetic writer, you refrain from passing judgment on other people's ideas. Don't begin an argument with an attack but with an acknowledgement that there might be different views. Alternatively, you might start with a summary of recent research in the area and then branch off into your own specific angle. In this manner, you attempt to understand your audience, and the reader is not immediately threatened by the viewpoints.

Because the Rogerian method focuses on building connections between writer and reader, great emphasis is also placed on common values, beliefs, and opinions. To a certain extent, the "win–win" concept is applicable because two overarching aspects of the style are negotiation and respect. While useful in all situations, this methodology is particularly valuable for educators as many of the discussions in this field deal with emotional and personal issues (student achievement, student placement, interpersonal relationships, etc.).

In some ways, educators must embrace the classical with the Rogerian. There are indeed times when one needs to be forceful; however, there are many other cases when it is necessary to achieve common ground for mutual growth. In the latter case, the Rogerian methodology provides a realistic framework.

The Rogerian Argument Model

The Rogerian argument model follows a basic three-tiered approach. In the first stage, you anticipate common ground with the reader and note that his or her view has some history and/or validity. For example, in a paper suggesting that homework is no longer necessary, you might begin by noting some of the supposed values of homework and even how some parents view it as a connecting vehicle to the school. In this example, you don't immediately alienate your audience but attempt to place the argument within a common framework.

In the next stage, the main body of the paper, you advance your argument. While you are free to agree or disagree with anything you read, you must do so in a professional manner. Therefore, be sure to avoid loaded and prejudicial language, vindictiveness, and sarcasm. There is no place for these elements in academic and professional writing. Even if you discern their use in the volume you're critiquing, you do not have licence to retaliate. Using such pointed language will also weaken your case.

You must also ensure that you critique the ideas, not the author. However, don't state (or even imply) that other positions are less moral or less ethical than the one being advocated. Instead, explain your positions clearly and use whatever research and other data necessary to support them. It is important that you state opposing views accurately and without emotion. You don't have to agree with another point of view to contrast it with your own, but you must understand it thoroughly. One quick way to lose a reader is to misrepresent or denigrate his or her view. We have all become annoyed when someone distorts our opinions. These kinds of misrepresentations make further dialogue and understanding difficult and often lead to lasting animosities.

The final stage is the conclusion, which tends to be short in the Rogerian method. State your thesis, one that may acknowledge opposing points of view but advocates a new orientation (i.e., the one about which you're writing). Again, it is important to present this conclusion without the use of volatile language or the attempt to destroy non-compliant points of view. This is not the win-at-all-costs argumentative style but one that shows respect for your opponents.

THE ACADEMIC CRITIQUE

While a professional summary is a targeted and restricted form, an academic critique can take on a life of its own. There are no percentage limits, no demands regarding direct quotations, and one's personal views are expected. Therefore, to a certain extent, the critique may be viewed as a summary with attitude. Even so, it is still important to remember the Rogerian approach and the rules about sarcasm and respect.

In academic and professional circles, educators give opinions all the time. However, these opinions must be based on research and/or experience. One's feelings are not normally germane to a professional discussion. Similarly, when commenting upon an article or book, your critique is expected to be based on reputable sources. You are expected to disagree with others and participate in the normal give-and-take that occurs within the academic world, but this exchange of ideas must be built upon past research, recognized methodology, and meaningful experiences.

An academic critique consists of several elements that can be adjusted as the need demands:

- introduction
- summary
- presentation

- personal response
- conclusion

The introduction includes author background and affiliations. Author information is important in the critique process because it places the article or book within an appropriate educational continuum. You will need to find information about the author's academic background, university and professional affiliations, and research and publishing history. This information is not judgmental in nature but simply exploratory. The Internet, particularly publisher and university or college websites, provides a wealth of information in this area.

Every academic critique contains a summary. Depending on how you intend to organize your critique, this component can appear at the beginning of the piece or be broken up and used as sections throughout the paper. The choice is yours, but it might be best to follow a somewhat simpler style by placing the summary after the author information. If you have already written a professional summary on the material, it can be easily inserted here; otherwise, you will engage in the summary process.

The next section specifically comments upon the author's research and data presentation. While you may have touched upon this aspect at some other point, it is essential to make it clear. Specifically, you want to include details regarding the accuracy of the information presented by the author: sample size, questions asked, interpretations, and specific arguments and conclusions that emanate from the methodology.

The use of direct quotations in an academic critique is usually necessary. The author will make seminal points that can sometimes be best portrayed by a direct quotation. Further, you should use quotations from other authors as both rebuttal and support. Unlike the professional summary, where the use of the author's own words is eschewed, the academic critique is the place to juxtapose your writing with that of others.

The last two components of the academic critique are where you, as an evolving educator, can make a stance. Your personal views are appropriate and can easily be included, especially if you can assert a kind of mini-expert role. For example, you can make direct and supportive assertions by drawing on your own personal and professional experiences. Depending on the topic under review, you can intervene. If the article deals with the use of homework, you can recollect your own feelings about the subject. If the volume looks at classroom management regimes, you can make an observation based on your own experiences.

An academic critique must have a conclusion. As previously stated, some people find writing conclusions difficult. Do you rehash what has already been stated or offer new criticisms? Generally speaking, a conclusion at this level is one or two paragraphs that wrap up the main issues, state the overarching criticisms, and attempt to provide a dénouement to your work.

SUMMARY

As a student and as an educator, you will constantly write for different audiences with varying points of view. You may also need to present opinions that you know are not held by your audience. Therefore, it is essential that you develop a range of professional and academic writing strategies and become confident in writing several forms, such as the professional summary and academic critique.

REFERENCES

Rogers, C. R. (1980). *A way of being*. New York, NY: Houghton Mifflin.

Rosenblatt, L. M. (1995). *Literature as exploration* (5th ed.). New York, NY: Modern Language Association of America.

CHAPTER 4

Writing Book Reviews and Other Kinds of Reports

OBJECTIVES

- To understand the purpose of reviews and reports
- To identify the audience for the review or report
- To understand the need to be clear in thought and prose
- To recognize that follow-up may be necessary

INTRODUCTION

Educators write reviews and reports all the time. As a teacher, you will be asked to comment on books as possible class texts, or you may serve on a school library committee and compile a compendium of suggested titles or perhaps just keep a personal book-review file. Throughout your career, you will also be asked to provide reports on any number of activities, such as an incident report detailing a schoolyard accident, a written commentary of a parent–teacher meeting, or an opinion piece to your principal regarding a potential class trip.

The following guidelines cover the three main types of book reports (informative, analytic, and literary) and point out their main characteristics. Each type serves a different purpose and requires you to make different judgments. These features can also be applied to the other kinds of reports that will become part of your professional writing.

THE INFORMATIVE REPORT

The purpose of an *informative report* is to summarize a book briefly and coherently. It is not intended to be evaluative. That is, it says nothing about your reaction to the work—no personal comments, judgments, recommendations, or criticism of the characters, arguments, or quality of writing. Using examples and data from the text, it simply records, as accurately and concisely as possible, your understanding of what the author has written. It's not a complicated task, but it does call on your ability to get to the heart of things and to highlight the most salient elements, to separate what is important from what is not. Aside from some pertinent publication information, all a simple informative report needs to be is an exact summary of the book's contents.

The basic tenets of the informative report are replicated in certain educational settings, such as recounting a meeting with parents or reviewing a workshop. In other words, these accounts should also be as precise and neutral as possible. Even if you are an active participant in the process, you should write as if you were a court reporter, impartially recording the scene.

Reading the Book

DETERMINE THE AUTHOR'S PURPOSE

An author writes a book or an article for a reason. Usually it is to cast some new light on a subject, propose a new theory, or bring together the existing knowledge in a field. You must discover the author's purpose if you want to understand what guided his or her selection and arrangement of material. The best way to find out what the author intends to do is to check the table of contents, preface, and introduction.

SKIM THE BOOK FIRST

A quick overview of a book's contents will show you what the author considers most important and what kind of evidence he or she presents. The details will be much more understandable once you know where the book as a whole is going.

REREAD CAREFULLY AND TAKE NOTES

A second, more thorough reading will be the basis of your note-taking. Since you have already determined the relative importance that the author gives to various ideas, you can be selective and avoid getting bogged down in less important details. Just be sure that you don't neglect any crucial passages or controversial claims.

When taking notes, try to condense the ideas. Don't take them down word for word or simply paraphrase them. You will have a much firmer grasp of the material if you resist the temptation to quote; force yourself to interpret and summarize. This approach will also help you make your report concise. Remember, you want to be brief as well as clear. Condensing the material as you take notes will ensure that your report is a true summary, not just a string of quotations or paraphrases.

Writing the Report

IDENTIFY PRIMARY AND SECONDARY IDEAS
When writing your report, give the same relative emphasis to each area as the author does. Don't just list the topics in the book or the conclusions reached; discriminate between primary ideas and secondary ones.

FOLLOW THE BOOK'S ORDER OF PRESENTATION
A simple summary doesn't have to address topics in the same order in which they are presented in the book, but it's usually safer to follow the author's lead. That way your summary will be a clear reflection of the original.

FOLLOW THE LOGICAL CHAIN OF THE ARGUMENTS
Don't leave any confusing holes in your summary. You won't be able to cover every detail, of course, but you must make sure to trace all the main arguments in such a way that they make sense.

INCLUDE THE KEY EVIDENCE SUPPORTING THE AUTHOR'S ARGUMENTS
Remember to include the evidence the author uses to support his or her arguments. Without some supporting details, your reader will have no way of assessing the strength of the author's conclusions.

TAILOR THE LENGTH TO FIT YOUR NEEDS
A summary can be any length, but it is perhaps best to keep in mind two general guidelines: (1) never exceed 10 per cent of the original work in your summary, and (2) most academic book reports range from 800 to 1,500 words. If the report is an assignment, find out how long your instructor wants it to be. If it's for personal reference only, you will have to decide how much detail you want to have on hand.

READ AND REVISE YOUR REPORT TO MAKE SURE IT'S COHERENT
Summaries can often seem choppy or disconnected because so much of the original material is left out. Use linking words and phrases to help create a flow and give your writing a sense of logical development. Careful paragraph division will also help to frame the various sections of the summary.

EDIT YOUR REPORT CAREFULLY
You may find that you have to edit your work a number of times to eliminate unnecessary words and get your report down to the required length. Editing can be a difficult task, but it becomes easier with practice.

INCLUDE PUBLICATION DETAILS
Details about the book (publisher, place and date of publication, and number of pages) must appear somewhere in your report, whether at the beginning or at the end. Use American Psychological Association (APA) or Chicago style throughout (see Chapter 6).

THE ANALYTIC REPORT

In many ways, an *analytic report* is an informative report with personality. That is, it not only summarizes the main ideas but also evaluates them based on your professional experiences and/or knowledge of other authoritative writings. It's best to begin with an introduction and then follow with a summary and an evaluation. Publication details are usually listed at the beginning, but can be placed at the end.

Introduction

The introduction provides all the background information necessary for a reader who is unfamiliar with the book. Here are some of the questions you might consider:

- What is the book about? Is the title pertinent and useful as a guide to the book's contents?
- What is the author's purpose? What kind of audience is he or she writing for? How is the topic limited? Is the central theme or argument stated or only implied?
- How does this book relate to others in the same field?
- What is the author's background and reputation? What other books or articles has he or she written?

- Are there any special circumstances connected with the writing of this book? For example, was it written with the co-operation of particular scholars or institutions? Does the subject have special significance for the author?
- What kind of evidence does the author present to support his or her ideas? Is it reliable and current?

Not all of these questions will apply to every book and every situation, but an introduction that answers some of them will put your reader in a much better position to appreciate what you have to say in your evaluation.

Summary

You cannot analyze or professionally comment on a book without discussing its contents. The basic steps are the same as those of the informative report. You may present a condensed version of the book's contents as a separate section, followed by your evaluation, or you may integrate the two, assessing the author's arguments as you present them.

Evaluation

In evaluating the book, you will want to consider some of the following questions:

- How is the book organized? Does the author focus too much on some areas and too little on others? Has anything been left out?
- How has the author divided the work into chapters? Are the divisions valid? Do the chapter titles accurately reflect each chapter's contents?
- What kind of assumptions does the author make in presenting the material? Are they stated or implied? Are they valid?
- Does the author accomplish what he or she sets out to do? Does the author's position change during the course of the book? Are there any contradictions or weak spots in the arguments? Does the author recognize those weaknesses or omissions?
- What documentation does the author provide to support the central theme or argument? Is it reliable and current? Is any of the evidence distorted or misinterpreted? Could the same evidence be used to support a different case? Does the author leave out any important evidence that might weaken his or her case? Is the author's position convincing?

- Does the author agree or disagree with other writers who have dealt with the same material or problem? In what respects?
- Is the book clearly written and interesting to read? Is the writing repetitious? Too detailed? Not detailed enough? Is the style clear? Or is it plodding, jargonistic, or flippant?
- Does the book raise issues that need further exploration? Does it present any challenges or leave unfinished business for the author or other scholars to pursue?
- If the book has an index, how good is it?
- Are there illustrations? Are they helpful?
- To what extent would you recommend this book? What effect has it had on you?

Remember that your job is not to interpret the content of the book but to indicate its strengths and weaknesses. Also, be sure that you review the book the author actually wrote, not the one you wish he or she had written. In short, be fair. Even if you find a work wanting, it is not your place to become a vicious reviewer. Just as criticism can be given to colleagues and students in a kind and respectful manner, you must also temper your comments with consideration.

THE LITERARY REVIEW

The *literary review* is a variation of the analytic book report. Although literature is its most frequent subject, it may deal with a wide range of topics, from art and music to the social sciences. The term *literary* refers to the style of the review rather than to the material discussed; the review should stand on its own merit as an attractive piece of writing.

The literary review is important for educators, and many of you will be called upon to handle student artistic endeavours. These literary avenues run the gamut from student plays to museum trips, school newspapers, and even original, in-house presentations. Having the skills required for a literary review will help you report and comment on these projects.

The advantage of a literary review is the freedom that it allows you in content, style, and form. You may emphasize any aspect you like, as long as you leave your reader with a basic understanding of what the book is about. Remember that your job is not to give a plot summary. In most cases, your purpose is simply to provide a graceful introduction to the work based on your personal assessment of its most intriguing—or annoying—features. Be careful, though, not to make it too personal; some reviewers tell us more about themselves than about the book. Although a literary review is usually less comprehensive than an analytic report, it should always be thoughtful, and your judgment must never be superficial.

The best way of learning how to write good literary reviews is to read some of them. Check the book review sections of a magazine such as *Maclean's* or the weekend edition of *The Globe and Mail* to see different approaches. Pay particular attention to the various techniques that reviewers use to catch the reader's interest and hold it. The basic rule is to reinforce your comments with specific details from the book; concrete examples will add authenticity and life to your review.

OTHER KINDS OF REPORTS

Sometimes referred to as memos, various other reports make up a significant part of a teacher's writing. Along with those already mentioned, these forms might also include completing a report on a student teacher assigned to your classroom, challenging the location and date for the annual field day, responding to a curriculum proposal from a group of parents, or suggesting an alternate school schedule so as to extend an off-campus event. Any time a colleague, unit head, senior administrator, or parent asks you for a written comment, review, follow-up, or reaction to a topic, you would be wise to use an appropriate style and form. A well-crafted report will go a long way in helping you make your case in a serious and professional manner. Over time and with experience, you will become proficient at writing these observations. In a sense, this kind of professional writing will also prepare you for one of the most important forms of educational writing: the report card (see Chapter 9).

CHAPTER 5

Using Illustrations

OBJECTIVES

- To explore the use of illustrations to enhance your writing
- To utilize various media to your best advantage
- To exercise care in the use of all visuals

INTRODUCTION

People are accustomed to seeing and interpreting visual representations of ideas. From international traffic symbols to corporate logos, visual symbols and illustrations are part of our everyday lives. Our increasing reliance on the visual may result in part from the influence of television and the Internet. This dependence also reflects the multicultural nature of our society and the need to communicate ideas quickly with images and symbols that transcend linguistic and cultural barriers.

Contemporary computer programs, which typically operate on a graphic interface, make it easy to create, format, and annotate illustrations. This visual representation of information allows us to see points quickly and in a larger scheme. At the same time, it can weaken academic papers if used without careful thought and planning. Just as one can become confused or distracted by highway signs or too much noise, written works can lose impact if they are overloaded with visuals, especially if the illustrations are overly complex and technical.

In your writing projects, you must decide whether using an illustration is appropriate and, if so, which type will best present the relevant information. This chapter will provide you with guidelines on when to use illustrations, particularly tables, charts, and photographs, and how to use them successfully.

BASIC GUIDELINES

Especially when writing reports, consider whether you can display some of your information visually. Here are a few basic guidelines for using visual aids effectively:

- Information in an illustration must expand on or complement information in the text, not simply duplicate it. For example, if you have a paragraph describing sliding success rates in a grade 7 mathematics examination, don't simply rehash the same information in a chart or table.
- Simple illustrations are much better than cluttered and complicated ones. The easier it is for the reader to grasp the information quickly and accurately, the better.
- As in the use of headings and subheadings in any written submission, make the title of the visual specifically reflect the point of the illustration, not just the topic. Be specific about the content; for example, *Ontario Education Market: Declining Employment Figures for 2012* is better than *Education Figures*.
- You must refer to every illustration in the text, explaining why it is there and/or what it shows. It is inadvisable to insert a visual without making its place and purpose germane to your writing. If you have several visuals, number each one so that you can refer to them all clearly (e.g., "As Figure 1 shows . . .").
- Any illustration taken from another source must be referenced appropriately. Normally, you can freely use such material in a university or college project. However, if it is copyrighted and your project will have a wider circulation (such as within a school board or an education journal), you may need to obtain the copyright holder's permission to use the illustration. Visuals that you have created do not require referencing or permission, unless you have published them elsewhere or they are based on someone else's work or data.

TABLES

A table can convey a large amount of information, both numerical and textual, without losing detail (see Table 5.1). If you are giving specific information in numerical form, a table allows you to show precise data more clearly than a chart does. It is the sensible choice when the data is too detailed or too complex

Table 5.1   Enrolment Increase in Black Elm District School Board

School	September 2011 Enrolment	September 2012 Enrolment	Change (+/−)
W. L. Mackenzie Elementary	580	625	+ 45
Waterside Elementary	455	482	+ 27
Black Elm Elementary	716	754	+ 38
Maple Tree Middle School	843	938	+ 95
Black Elm High School	1,523	1,744	+221

to be clearly illustrated in a chart (such as when small differences in enrolment data are critical) or when some or all of the information is text based.

CHARTS

Although they aren't quite as precise as tables, charts can dramatize information more effectively and are easier for the reader to grasp. Computer programs offer a wide range of chart types, but here are three of the most common.

Line Charts

A *line chart* (see Figure 5.1) shows change over a period of time. As such, it's often used to point out trends or fluctuations, as in academic success or drop-out rates. In devising a line chart, put quantities on the vertical axis and time values on the horizontal. Try to shape the dimensions of the graph to give the most accurate impression of the extent of change. Never distort your graph to emphasize a point—for instance, by shortening the horizontal axis and lengthening the vertical to make a gradual rise look more dramatic. Doing so will only reduce your credibility and cause your reader to question the reliability of your information and the validity of your arguments.

Bar Charts

A *bar chart*, such as the one in Figure 5.2, is used to compare elements at fixed points in time. You might use a bar chart to show the book costs associated with school libraries over a particular year or from one year to the next. The bars can be horizontal or vertical, depending on the range of data, and they can be segmented to show different parts of the whole. Bars can also be grouped to compare one category with another.

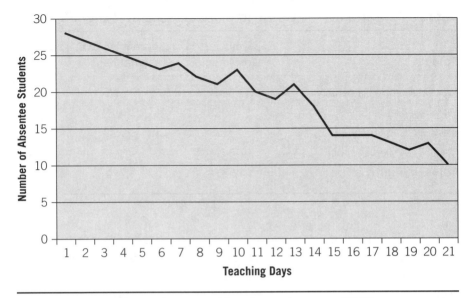

Figure 5.1   Grade 5 Absentee Numbers, January 2012

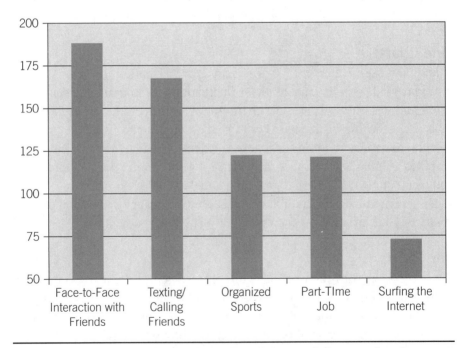

Figure 5.2   Top Five After-School Activities of the Graduating
Class, 2013

Pie Charts

A *pie chart* is used to emphasize proportions, to draw attention to the relative size of the parts that make up a whole. For example, it can provide a quick visual comparison of individual success rates in a school by gender, ethnic background, socio-economic status, etc. With a pie chart, you can also show percentages and separate one piece from the rest of the pie for emphasis, as in Figure 5.3.

TABLES OR CHARTS?

When deciding whether to use a table or a chart to present your data, you must always consider which will be the most effective in getting your point across. Tables have the advantage of being more exact than charts because they provide precise numerical information. They can also include text. On the other hand, charts often give a more compelling impression of the overall pattern of results.

In general, a table is a good choice if you have several sets of numbers that could get buried if you just listed them in the text. However, if you have

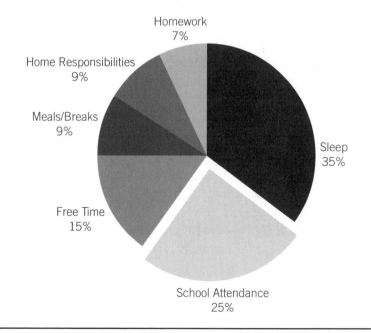

Figure 5.3   Average Time Lakeview School Grade 7 Students Spend on Daily Activities, 2010–2012

statistics for a number of conditions that vary systematically, a chart is the best way to illustrate the information. However, the choice between a table and a chart often comes down to nothing more than personal style or preference.

PHOTOGRAPHS

There is no question that "a picture is worth a thousand words." Therefore, the strategic insertion of a powerful photograph can make a significant point. If appropriate, photographs can also make research papers artistically appealing. However, depending on the kind of photograph being used, colour and print quality could be an issue.

When considering using photographs, recall the copyright guideline discussed earlier. Every photograph from an outside source must be referenced. There are also various laws regarding the use of personal photographs. For example, if you were researching the effectiveness of playground equipment, you might not be able to use photographs taken at the local park.

DANGERS IN USING ILLUSTRATIONS

As we have indicated throughout this chapter, there are some hazards involved in using illustrations. Keep the following in mind for your writing projects:

- Computer programs can add visual impact and even drama to your written material, but they also make it tempting to add so much detail that you obscure the facts. Be sure that the designs you create are not too elaborate for your purpose. Visuals are not meant to dazzle but to make it easier for the reader to understand the information.
- Any illustration, even if it is created on a computer, can distort information. For instance, the slope of a graph line can be made to look steep or shallow, even with the same data; trend lines can begin at a time that omits unfavourable periods. Although line and bar charts are the most susceptible to distortion, the shapes and proportions of other diagrams can also give a false picture. Be careful to present as accurate a picture as possible so that your illustrations reinforce the credibility of your words.
- While colour can be effective in charts, especially ones that include several indicators, be careful not to overuse it. Where possible, keep to the standard grayscale of most printers.

CHAPTER 6

Documenting Sources

OBJECTIVES

- To avoid plagiarism in professional and academic writing
- To understand appropriate documentation procedures
- To explore APA and Chicago styles, the two main citation methods in educational writing
- To write an annotated bibliography

INTRODUCTION

Much of your writing will require you to consult secondary sources, such as books and articles, to become familiar with current research and to find support for your ideas. It's essential to acknowledge those sources, not only when you quote directly from them but also when you restate, in your own words, arguments or ideas taken from them. If you don't cite them, your reader will assume that the words, ideas, or thoughts are yours. In other words, you're plagiarizing, and the penalties can be severe.

The purpose of documentation is not only to avoid charges of plagiarism but also to show the body of knowledge upon which your own work is built. Academic writing is based on the premise that educators and researchers are not working in a vacuum but are indebted to those academics and scholars who came before them. By documenting your sources, you are showing that you understand this concept and are ready to make your own contribution to the body of knowledge in your field. Proper documentation also gives your readers the information they need to access what you have read.

GENERAL CONSIDERATIONS REGARDING THE USE OF QUOTATIONS

Because some of your documentation will concern direct quotations, let's first look at ways to include them in your writing. Judicious use of quotations can add authority to your writing as well as help you avoid charges of plagiarism, but you must use quotations with care. Never quote a passage just because it sounds impressive; be sure that it really adds to your discussion, either by expressing an idea with special force or cogency or by giving substance to a debatable point. The following are some general guidelines for incorporating quotations in your work as running text:

1. Integrate the quotation so that it makes sense in the context of your discussion and fits grammatically into a sentence:

   ✗ Whether Dr Joseph Smith is a visionary is debatable. "Physical libraries will be obsolete within a decade" (Smith, 2001, p. 354) is now highly ironic.

   ✓ Whether Dr Joseph Smith is a visionary is debatable. His prediction that "physical libraries will be obsolete within a decade" (Smith 2001, 354) is now highly ironic.

   Note that the first example is acknowledged using the American Psychological Association (APA) method and the second with Chicago, the two styles used most often in educational writing.

2. If the quotation is less than a full sentence, include it as part of your text and enclose it in quotation marks. If the quotation is longer, set it as a block of free-standing text. In APA style, a quotation of more than 40 words should be set as a block quotation. Chicago style sets excerpts of more than 100 words in this manner. If the quotation consists of more than one paragraph, indent the first line of the second and subsequent paragraphs an additional three spaces.

3. Be accurate. Reproduce the exact wording, punctuation, and spelling of the original, including any and all errors. You must never edit or modify a direct quotation in any way; however, you can acknowledge a typo or mistake in the original by inserting the Latin word *sic* in square brackets within the quotation or in parentheses after the quotation. If you want to italicize part of the quotation for emphasis, add "my emphasis" or

"emphasis added" in square brackets within the quotation or in parentheses after the quotation. If you want to insert an explanatory comment of your own into a quotation, enclose it in square brackets.

4. If you want to omit something from the original text, use ellipses (see pages 168–9).

CITATIONS AND REFERENCES

A citation is a brief notation embedded within the text that indicates, as a form of shorthand, where a quotation or major idea originated. Unlike endnotes and footnotes, which can be cumbersome and require your audience to stop reading to see the reference, citations do not interrupt the reading process.

Citations acknowledge that you have incorporated another's words, but they do not supply complete information. The full reference, which supplies the exact location of the cited material, appears at the end of your written piece in a bibliography or a reference or works cited list. A bibliography (from the Greek word *bibliographia*, meaning "book writing") is an alphabetical list of sources that have been read. In a sense, a bibliography can encompass a vast inventory of material, as it is possible to maintain a list of every source that one has ever read on a given topic. A reference or works-cited list, on the other hand, is a much shorter list that includes only the sources referred to in the paper. In most of your professional and academic papers, you will use citations and a reference list.

DOCUMENTING YOUR SOURCES

The documentation style you use in your writing will depend on the preference of your instructor, department, or employer. Begin a writing assignment by finding out if there is a preferred documentation style and set of guidelines. If there isn't, use either the APA or Chicago style as described in the following sections. Keep in mind that you must be consistent in any given paper and use only one style throughout. Further, these styles are exact. The placement of such elements as parentheses and commas and the use of italics are important. Such detail may seem tedious, but it allows for clarity and precision in your documentation. Another point to remember is that style guides are constantly undergoing revision, especially with the wealth of online information currently available. It's always safest to check the latest editions of the relevant manual or website to be sure that you have the most updated information.

APA STYLE

In 1929, the APA established a set of submission guidelines for their journals. This documentation style, which uses parenthetical citations within the text keyed to a reference list, is the one most commonly used in the social sciences (including education), business, and nursing. It is also the style used in this book.

 For more detailed information, consult the *Publication Manual of the American Psychological Association* (2010) or visit the APA website (http://apastyle.apa.org/).

In-Text Citations

BOOK OR ARTICLE WITH ONE AUTHOR

If the author's name is given in the text, cite only the year of publication in parentheses. Otherwise, give both the author's surname and the year, separated by a comma:

> Sockett (2008) presents four teaching models in his discussion of teacher education.

> The number of male teachers in Canada increased by more than 25 per cent between 1920 and the early 1980s (Wotherspoon, 2004).

BOOK OR ARTICLE WITH MORE THAN ONE AUTHOR

If the work you are citing has two authors, include both names every time you cite the reference in the text. Use an ampersand (&) when the names are in parentheses but *and* in the text:

> Respect for classmates is considered a common feature of successful students (Goldstein & Brooks, 2007).

> Goldstein and Brooks (2007) include respect for classmates as a common feature of successful students.

If there are three, four, or five authors, cite all the names when the reference first occurs and afterwards cite only the first author, followed by "et al.":

> Howley, Wood, and Hough (2011) studied technology integration in rural elementary schools. . . . Research shows that rural teachers are more positive about technology integration than urban teachers are (Howley et al., 2011).

In every citation of a work with six or more authors, cite only the surname of the first, followed by "et al."

BOOK OR ARTICLE WITH A GROUP OR CORPORATE AUTHOR

Corporations, associations, and government agencies serving as authors are usually given in full each time they appear. Some group authors may be given in full the first time and abbreviated in subsequent citations if doing so provides the reader with enough information to easily locate the entry in the reference list:

> One article examines the diversity of university teachers in Canada (Canadian Association of University Teachers [CAUT], 2010). . . . The same article concludes that Aboriginal peoples remain the most under-represented group among Canadian university professors (CAUT, 2010).

As a general rule, always spell out an abbreviation the first time it is used. Don't assume that your readers will know the same abbreviations that you do. Once the full title has been used, the short form can then safely take its place.

ARTICLE WITH NO KNOWN OR DECLARED AUTHOR

If the work you are referencing has no known or declared author, cite the first few words of the title as well as the year:

> Research indicates that a student's fitness level could affect his or her academic performance ("Why Couch Potatoes," 2012).

In this case, the full title of the article is "Why Couch Potatoes Are More Likely to Do Poorly in School."

SPECIFIC PARTS OF A SOURCE

If you are referring to a particular part of a source, you must indicate the page, chapter, figure, table, and/or equation. Always give page numbers for quotations:

(Smith 2000, p. 1148)

(Alon 2009, pp. 731–55)

(Robertson, 1998, Chapter 2)

(Edmunds & Edmunds, 2010, Table 2.2)

Note that APA prefaces page numbers with "p." for a single page and "pp." for several pages.

ELECTRONIC SOURCES

It is becoming increasingly common for educators to use electronic sources in their writing. In-text citations for electronic sources use the same formatting principles as print sources. However, when an electronic source does not include information to identify its exact location, the following exceptions apply:

- If your source has no page numbers, use the paragraph number or section number (if one is available), preceded by the paragraph symbol or the abbreviation "para.":

  (Alberta Education, 2008, para. 1)

- If sections, pages, and paragraphs are not numbered, cite the heading and the number of the next paragraph:

  (Council for Exceptional Children [CEC], 2006, Memory, para. 6)

- If you are citing an entire website, include only the URL in the text:

  The Canadian School Boards Association website (http://cdnsba.org/) . . .

References

Entries in an APA reference list adhere to the following guidelines:

- Entries begin with the author's surname, followed by his or her initials; full given names are not used.
- For works with multiple authors, all names are reversed; the name of the last author is preceded by an ampersand (&) rather than *and*.
- The date of publication appears immediately after the authors' names, in parentheses.
- Entries for different works by the same author are listed in reverse chronological order (i.e., older date first). Two or more works by the same author with the same publication date/year are arranged alphabetically by title.
- For titles of books and articles, only proper nouns and the first word of the title and subtitle (if there is one) are capitalized.

- Titles of articles or selections in books are not enclosed in quotation marks.

BOOK WITH ONE AUTHOR

Earl, L. (2003). *Assessment as learning: Using classroom assessment to maximize learning.* Thousand Oaks, CA: Corwin Press.

BOOK WITH MORE THAN ONE AUTHOR

King, A. J. C., & Peart, M. J. (1992). *Teachers in Canada: Their work and quality of life.* Ottawa, Canada: Canadian Teachers' Federation.

For books with eight or more authors, list only the first six, followed by an ellipsis and the name of the last author.

BOOK WITH A GROUP OR CORPORATE AUTHOR

Ontario Ministry of Education. (2004). *The individualized education plan (IEP): A resource guide.* Toronto, Canada: Queen's Printer for Ontario.

BOOK WITH AN EDITOR

Portelli, J. P., & Solomon, R. P. (Eds.). 2001. *The erosion of democracy in education.* Calgary, Canada: Detselig.

SELECTION IN AN EDITED BOOK

Rogers, A. G. (1998). Understanding changes in girls' relationships and in ego development: Three studies of adolescent girls. In P. M. Westenberg, A. Blasi, & L. D. Cohen (Eds.), *Personality development: Theoretical, empirical, and clinical investigations of Loevinger's conception of ego development* (pp. 145–162). Hillsdale, NJ: Erlbaum.

Note that the page numbers of the selection are given, preceded by "pp."

ARTICLE IN A JOURNAL

Bell, S. K., & Morgan, S. B. (2000). Children's attitudes and behavioral intentions toward a peer presented as obese: Does a medical explanation for the obesity make a difference? *Journal of Pediatric Psychology, 25,* 137–146.

Note that the page numbers of the article are given but, unlike entries for selections in books and newspaper articles, are not preceded by "pp."

When a journal has continuous pagination, the issue number should not be included. If each issue begins on page 1, give the issue number in parentheses before the page numbers and immediately following the volume number, with no punctuation separating them and a comma following the closing bracket. The volume number is italicized; the issue number and the parentheses are not:

> Graham, C., & New, D. (2004). Standardized testing and the construction of governable persons. *Journal of Curriculum Studies, 36*(3), 295–319.

ARTICLE IN A NEWSPAPER

> Fine, S. (2001, August 27). Schools told to fix boys' low grades. *The Globe and Mail*, pp. A1, A7.

When a newspaper or magazine article continues on a non-consecutive page, the first page is given, followed by a comma and the page(s) it continues on.

For an unsigned newspaper article, begin the entry with the title. If the previous example did not include an author's name, the entry would look like this:

> Schools told to fix boys' low grades. (2001, August 27). *The Globe and Mail*, pp. A1, A7.

ARTICLE IN A MAGAZINE

> Hoffman, J. (2012, March). Bringing empathy into the classroom. *Today's Parent*, 59.

If the magazine has a volume number, it should be included in italics after the magazine title. For monthly or bi-monthly magazines, give the month(s) in full; for weekly magazines, give the month (in full) and day.

LECTURE OR PRESENTATION

> Krasnow, M. (2008, June). Evolutionizing the study of conceptual knowledge. Paper presented at Human Behavior and Evolution Society 2008, Kyoto, Japan.

ELECTRONIC SOURCES

Include the same elements as you would for print sources and add any electronic retrieval information that will help guide readers to the source. A significant feature of the sixth edition of the *Publication Manual* is the inclusion of new guidelines for referencing electronic sources, with emphasis on the *digital object identifier (DOI) system* of tracking digital information. Because links can be unstable, a registration agency assigns a DOI to each article to identify it and provide a means of electronic retrieval. This identifier is a unique alphanumeric string that begins with a 10 and contains a prefix and suffix separated by a slash (e.g. 10.1037/0096-3445). The DOI typically appears near the copyright notice on the first page of the article.

APA style includes the following guidelines for tracking electronic sources:

- Include DOIs in references when they are available; no further retrieval information (e.g., URL) is required.
- If no DOI is available, write "Retrieved from" and give the URL of the journal's or publisher's homepage. You should provide an exact URL if it will take your reader to the relevant material more reliably.
- Give the retrieval date only in cases where the information is likely to be changed or updated; no retrieval date is necessary for journal articles or books.
- For most documents accessed through electronic databases, the database name is no longer a necessary element of the reference.
- If you need to break an URL, do so before most punctuation rather than using a hyphen. Don't add a period after the DOI or URL.

JOURNAL ARTICLE WITH DOI

Stevenson, J., & Clegg, S. (2010). Possible selves: Students orientating themselves towards the future through extracurricular activity. *British Educational Research Journal, 37*(2), 231–246. doi:10.1080/01411920903540672

JOURNAL ARTICLE WITH NO DOI

Jull, S. (2000). Youth violence, schools, and the management question: A discussion of zero tolerance and equity in public schooling. *Canadian Journal of Educational Administration and Policy*. Retrieved from http://www.umanitoba.ca/publications/cjeap/articles/jull.html

ONLINE DICTIONARY

Homework. (n.d.). In *Merriam-Webster's online dictionary*. Retrieved from http://www.merriam-webster.com/dictionary/homework

ONLINE ENCYCLOPEDIA

Phillips, D. C. (2009). Philosophy of education. In E. N. Zalta (Ed.), *The Stanford encyclopedia of philosophy* (Spring 2009 ed.). Retrieved from http://plato.stanford.edu/archives/spr2009/entries/education-philosophy/

ONLINE NEWSPAPER ARTICLE

Arnold, R. (2012, June 7). Consequences lacking for poor student effort in high school. *The Vancouver Sun*. Retrieved from http://www.vancouversun.com/news/Consequences+lacking+poor+student+effort+high+school/6743388/story.html

VIDEO BLOG POST

Khan, S. (2011, March 9). Let's use video to reinvent education: Salman Khan on TED.com. [Video file]. Retrieved from http://blog.ted.com/2011/03/09/lets-use-video-to-reinvent-education-salman-khan-on-ted-com/

CHICAGO STYLE

The Chicago style is another standard used in educational writing. Developed by the University of Chicago Press in 1906, this style outlines two methods of documentation:

1. The *notes and bibliography* method, also known as the *humanities style*, is preferred by those in literature, history, and the arts. It uses superscript numerals to direct the reader to footnotes at the bottom of the page or endnotes on a separate page at the end of the document.
2. The *author–date* system, preferred in the physical, natural, and social sciences, follows the same principles as the APA style, with only minor stylistic differences.

 The Chicago Manual of Style (2010) provides detailed coverage of both methods. Another useful source is the online *Chicago-Style Citation*

Quick Guide (http://www.chicagomanualofstyle.org/tools_citationguide.html), which gives examples of references using the following system:

Notes and Bibliography: N = Note

B = Bibliography entry

Author–Date: T = In-text citation

R = Reference list entry

This system is also used in the following examples.

Book with One Author

N: 1.   Paul Axelrod, *Values in Conflict: The University, the Marketplace and the Trials of Liberal Education* (Montreal and Kingston: McGill-Queen's University Press, 2002), 47.

B: Axelrod, Paul. *Values in Conflict: The University, the Marketplace and the Trials of Liberal Education*. Montreal and Kingston: McGill-Queen's University Press, 2002.

T: (Axelrod 2002, 47)

R: Axelrod, Paul. 2002. *Values in Conflict: The University, the Marketplace and the Trials of Liberal Education*. Montreal and Kingston: McGill-Queen's University Press.

Book with More Than One Author

N: 1.   Maude Barlow and Heather-Jane Robertson, *Class Warfare: The Assault on Canada's Schools* (Toronto: Key Porter, 1994), 12.

B: Barlow, Maude, and Heather-Jane Robertson. *Class Warfare: The Assault on Canada's Schools*. Toronto: Key Porter, 1994.

T: (Barlow and Robertson 1994, 12)

R: Barlow, Maude, and Heather-Jane Robertson. 1994. *Class Warfare: The Assault on Canada's Schools*. Toronto: Key Porter.

Note that with four or more authors, notes and in-text references give just the first author, followed by "et al." The bibliography and reference list, however, list all authors' names.

Book with an Organization as Author

N: 1.   University of Chicago Press, *The Chicago Manual of Style*, 16th ed. (Chicago: University of Chicago Press, 2010), 656.

B: University of Chicago Press. *The Chicago Manual of Style*. 16th ed. Chicago: University of Chicago Press, 2010.

T: (University of Chicago Press 2010, 656)

R: University of Chicago Press. 2010. *The Chicago Manual of Style*. 16th ed. Chicago: University of Chicago Press.

Book with an Editor in Place of an Author

N: 1.   George Martell, ed., *The Politics of the Canadian Public School* (Toronto: James Lorimer, 1974), 60.

B: Martell, George, ed. *The Politics of the Canadian Public School*. Toronto: James Lorimer, 1974.

T: (Martell 1974, 60)

R: Martell, George, ed. 1974. *The Politics of the Canadian Public School*. Toronto: James Lorimer.

Book with an Editor or Translator in Addition to an Author

N: 1.   Jean Piaget, *The Psychology of Intelligence*, trans. Malcolm Piercy and D. E. Berlyne (London: Routledge, 2001), 188.

B: Piaget, Jean. *The Psychology of Intelligence*. Translated by Malcolm Piercy and D. E. Berlyne. London: Routledge, 2001.

T: (Piaget 2001, 188)

R: Piaget, Jean. 2001. *The Psychology of Intelligence*. Translated by Malcolm Piercy and D. E. Berlyne. London: Routledge.

CHAPTER OR OTHER PART OF A BOOK

N: 1. L. Nucci, "Classroom Management for Moral and Social Development," in *Handbook of Classroom Management: Research, Practice, and Contemporary Issues*, ed. C. M. Evertson and C. S. Weinstein (Mahwah, NJ: Lawrence Erlbaum, 2006), 722.

B: Nucci, L. "Classroom Management for Moral and Social Development." In *Handbook of Classroom Management: Research, Practice, and Contemporary Issues*, edited by C. M. Evertson and C. S. Weinstein, 711–34. Mahwah, NJ: Lawrence Erlbaum, 2006.

T: (Nucci 2006, 722)

R: Nucci, L. 2006. "Classroom Management for Moral and Social Development." In *Handbook of Classroom Management: Research, Practice, and Contemporary Issues*, edited by C.M. Evertson and C.S. Weinstein, 711–34. Mahwah, NJ: Lawrence Erlbaum.

Article in a Journal

N: 1. Lynn Isenbarger and Michalinos Zembylas, "The Emotional Labour of Caring in Teaching," *Teaching and Teacher Education* 22, no. 1 (2006): 133.

B: Isenbarger, Lynn, and Michalinos Zembylas. "The Emotional Labour of Caring in Teaching." *Teaching and Teacher Education* 22, no. 1 (2006): 120–34.

T: (Isenbarger and Zembylas 2006, 133)

R: Isenbarger, Lynn, and Michalinos Zembylas. 2006. "The Emotional Labour of Caring in Teaching." *Teaching and Teacher Education* 22 (2): 120–34.

Article in a Newspaper or Magazine

An article from a newspaper or magazine may be cited with a note or in-text citation and need not be included in a bibliography or reference list. If formal citation is required for some particular reason, follow these examples.

N: 1. Jay Teitel, "Failure to Fail," *The Walrus*, April 2008, 44.

B: Teitel, Jay. "Failure to Fail." *The Walrus*, April 2008.

T: (Teitel 2008, 44)

R: Teitel, Jay. 2008. "Failure to Fail." *The Walrus*, April 2008.

Article in an Online Journal

N: 1. Mohammad Zohrabi, "An Investigation of Curriculum Elements for the Enhancement of the Teaching–Learning Process," *Higher Education Studies* 1, no. 1 (June 2011): 68, doi:10.5539/hes.v1n1p67.

B: Zohrabi, Mohammad. "An Investigation of Curriculum Elements for the Enhancement of the Teaching–Learning Process." *Higher Education Studies* 1, no. 1 (June 2011): 67–78. doi:10.5539/hes.v1n1p67.

T: (Zohrabi 2011, 68)

R: Zohrabi, Mohammad. 2011. "An Investigation of Curriculum Elements for the Enhancement of the Teaching–Learning Process." *Higher Education Studies* 1, 1: 67–78. doi:10.5539/hes.v1n1p67.

If the article you're referencing does not have a DOI, include the URL.

WEBSITE OR WEBSITE CONTENT

A website may be cited in a note or running text (e.g., "CBC's website lists several . . ."). To cite content from a website, follow these examples. An access date, if required, is given in parentheses at the end of the citation. Note that websites and website content are often omitted from bibliographies and reference lists.

N: 1. "Education Funding Top of Alberta Teachers' Minds," *CBC News*, last updated May 21, 2012, http://origin.www.cbc.ca/news/polls/canadian-astronauts.html.

B: CBC. "Education Funding Top of Alberta Teachers' Minds." *CBC News*. Last updated May 21, 2012. http://origin.www.cbc.ca/news/polls/canadian-astronauts.html.

T: (CBC 2012)

R: CBC. 2012. "Education Funding Top of Alberta Teachers' Minds." *CBC News*. Last modified May 21. http://origin.www.cbc.ca/news/polls/canadian-astronauts.html.

Blog

Like websites, blogs are often cited in a note or running text only (e.g., "In a comment posted to *The Freshman* . . .") and are omitted from a bibliography or reference list. If you are required to provide more formal documentation, follow these examples. If an access date is required, include it in parentheses at the end of the citation.

N: 1. M. Crawford, July 30, 2009 (10:08 p.m.), comment on Noah Mazereeuw, "BC Government Cuts $16 million in Education Funding," *The Freshman* (blog), *Maclean's*, July 29, 2009. http://oncampus.macleans.ca/education/2009/07/29/bc-government-cuts-16-million-in-education-funding/.

B: *Freshman, The* (blog). *Maclean's*. http://oncampus.macleans.ca/education/category/blog-central/noah-mazereeuw/.

T: (Mazereeuw, 2009)

R: Mazereeuw, Noah. 2009. "BC Government Cuts $16 million in Education Funding." *The Freshman* (blog), July 29. *Maclean's*. http://oncampus.macleans.ca/education/category/blog-central/noah-mazereeuw/.

E-mail Message

As with websites and blogs, e-mail messages are usually cited in a note or running text only (e.g., "In an e-mail message to John Smith on May 28,

2008, Alex Hemmings stated . . .) and are omitted from a bibliography or reference list.

N: 1.   Alex Hemmings, e-mail message to John Smith, May 28, 2008.

LECTURE OR PAPER PRESENTED AT A MEETING

N: 1.   C. Noble, C. Rowland, and A. Chan, "Competition All the Way Down: How Children Learn Word Order Cues to Sentence Meaning" (paper presented at the 36th Annual Boston University Conference on Language Development, Boston, MA, November 4–6, 2011).

B: Noble, C., C. Rowland, and A. Chan. "Competition All the Way Down: How Children Learn Word Order Cues to Sentence Meaning." Paper presented at the 36th Annual Boston University Conference on Language Development, Boston, MA, November 4–6, 2011.

T: (Noble, Rowland, and Chan 2011)

R: Noble, C., C. Rowland, and A. Chan. 2011. "Competition All the Way Down: How Children Learn Word Order Cues to Sentence Meaning." Paper presented at the 36th Annual Boston University Conference on Language Development, November 4–6, in Boston, MA.

WRITING AN ANNOTATED BIBLIOGRAPHY

Some research assignments require an annotated bibliography, which is a standard list of sources accompanied by descriptive or evaluative comments on each item.

If you are asked for an annotated bibliography, begin by arranging your list of entries just as you would for a standard bibliography or reference list (i.e., alphabetically by author last name). Then include a brief comment about the source, for example, the quality of the information it contains, the approach of the author, a brief analysis of its strengths and/or weaknesses, or its relevance to your subject.

Depending on how much detail is required, the annotation can be as brief as a sentence or as long as several paragraphs. Many students keep an ongoing annotated bibliography while researching their papers. This practice is a solid way to keep track of what you have read and some information about each work.

Consult whatever style guide you are using for details about the specific format recommended for an annotated bibliography. The following is an example of a typical entry using APA format:

Kubiszyn, T., & Borich, G. (2009). Educational testing and measurement: *Classroom application and practice* (9th ed.). New York, NY: Wiley.

> An invaluable text for educators that includes various methods of measuring student progress. Provides current national policy on student evaluation and real examples.

REFERENCES

American Psychological Association. (2009). *Publication manual of the American Psychological Association* (6th ed.). Washington, DC: Author.

University of Chicago Press. (2010). *The Chicago manual of style: The essential guide for writers, editors, and publishers* (16th ed.). Chicago, IL: Author.

Writing with Style

INTRODUCTION

Writing with style does not mean inflating your prose with fancy or obscure words and extravagant images. Any style, from the simplest to the most elaborate, can be effective, depending on the occasion and intent. Writers known for their style are those who have projected their own personality into their writing; we can hear a distinctive voice in what they say. Obviously, it takes time to develop a unique style. To begin, you have to decide what general effect you want to create.

Taste in style reflects the times. In earlier centuries, many respected writers wrote in an elaborate style that we would consider much too wordy. Today, journalists have led the trend towards short, easy-to-grasp sentences and paragraphs. Writing in an academic context, you may expect your audience to be more reflective than the average newspaper reader, but the most effective style is still one that is clear, concise, and forceful.

BE CLEAR

Use Clear Diction

A current dictionary is a necessary investment. The dictionary you choose should offer both definitions and examples of word use. This reference tool will help you understand unfamiliar words or archaic and technical senses of common words. It will also help you with questions of spelling and usage. If you aren't sure if a particular word is too informal for your writing or if you have concerns that a certain word might be offensive, a good dictionary will give you this information.

You should be aware that Canadian usage and spelling may follow either British or American practice but usually combines aspects of both. In academic writing, Canadian and American spellings are accepted at equal value; however, do not mix variations within your paper. Whichever style you decide to follow, you must be consistent.

Another valuable reference is a thesaurus, which lists the synonyms and often the antonyms of words. This book can help when you want to avoid repeating yourself or when you are fumbling for a word that's on the tip of your tongue. Your word-processing program may also have a thesaurus feature. But be careful; make sure you distinguish between *denotative* and *connotative* meanings.

A word's denotation is its primary or "dictionary" meaning. Its connotations are any associations that it may suggest; they may not be as exact as the denotations, but they are part of the impression the word conveys. If you examine a list of synonyms in a thesaurus, you will see that even words with similar meanings can have dramatically different connotations. For example, your thesaurus may include the following synonyms for the word *indifferent: neutral, aloof, callous, moderate, unenthusiastic, apathetic, unprejudiced,* and *fair*. Imagine the different impressions these words would create in this sentence: "Questioned about the experiment's chance of success, he was _____ in his response." In order to write clearly, you must remember that a reader may react to the suggestive meaning of a word as much as to its dictionary meaning.

USE PLAIN ENGLISH

Plain words are almost always more forceful than fancy ones. For examples of plain English, think of the way you talk to your friends (apart from swearing and slang). Many of our most common words—the ones that sound most natural and direct—are short. A good number of them are also among the oldest words in the English language. By contrast, most words derived from other languages are longer and more complicated; even those that have been used for centuries can sound artificial. For this reason you should beware of words loaded with prefixes (*pre-*, *post-*, *anti-*, *pro-*, *sub-*, *maxi-*, etc.) and suffixes (*-ate*, *-ize*, *-tion*, etc.). These Latinate attachments can make individual words more precise and efficient, but putting a lot of them together will make your writing seem dense and hard to understand. In many cases you can substitute a plain word for a fancy one:

Fancy	Plain
accomplish	do
cognizant	aware
commence	begin, start
conclusion	end
determinant	cause
fabricate	build
finalize	finish, complete
firstly	first
infuriate	anger
maximization	increase
modification	change
numerous	many
obviate	prevent
oration	speech
prioritize	rank
remuneration	pay
requisite	needed
sanitize	clean
subsequently	later
systematize	order
terminate	end
transpire	happen
utilize	use

Suggesting that you write in plain English does not mean that you should never pick an unfamiliar word or foreign derivative. Sometimes those words are the only ones that will convey precisely what you mean. Inserting an unusual expression into a passage of plain writing can also be an effective means of catching the reader's attention—as long as you don't do it too often.

AVOID FANCY JARGON
All academic subjects have their own *jargon*, terminology that may be unfamiliar to outsiders but helps specialists explain things to each other. The

trouble is that people sometimes use jargon unnecessarily, thinking it will make them seem more knowledgeable. Too often, the result is not clarity but complication. The principle is easy: use specialized terminology only when it's a kind of shorthand that will help you explain something more precisely and efficiently. If plain prose will do just as well, use plain prose.

If it is necessary to use specialized words and phrases, make sure that they are clearly defined and explained the first time they are used in the paper. You cannot assume that the reader will have the same understanding of these technical words as you do.

BE PRECISE

Always be as specific as you can. Avoid all-purpose adjectives such as *major*, *significant*, and *important* and vague verbs such as *involve*, *entail*, and *exist* when you can be more specific:

orig. Donald Smith <u>was involved</u> in the construction of the CPR.

rev. Donald Smith <u>helped finance</u> the construction of the CPR.

Here's another example:

orig. The Canada–US Free Trade Agreement was a <u>significant</u> legacy of Brian Mulroney's years as prime minister.

rev. The Canada–US Free Trade Agreement was a <u>costly</u> legacy of Brian Mulroney's years as prime minister.

(or)

rev. The Canada–US Free Trade Agreement was a <u>beneficial</u> legacy of Brian Mulroney's years as prime minister.

AVOID UNNECESSARY QUALIFIERS

Qualifiers such as *very*, *rather*, and *extremely* are overused. Saying that something is *very beautiful* may have less impact than saying simply that it is *beautiful*. For example, compare these sentences:

That is a <u>beautiful</u> garden.

That is an <u>extremely beautiful</u> garden.

Which has more impact? When you think that an adjective needs quali-fying—and sometimes it will—first see if it's possible to change either the adjective or the phrasing. Instead of writing

Multinational Drugs made a very big profit last year,

write a precise statement:

Multinational Drugs made an <u>unprecedented</u> profit last year,

or (if you aren't sure whether or not the profit actually set a record):

Multinational Drugs had a profit <u>increase of 40 per cent</u> last year.

In some cases, qualifiers not only weaken your writing but are also redundant because the adjectives themselves are absolutes. To say that something is *very unique* makes as little sense as saying that someone is *slightly pregnant* or *extremely dead*.

Create Clear Paragraphs

Paragraphs come in so many sizes and patterns that no single formula could possibly cover them all. The two basic principles to remember are that

1. a paragraph is a means of developing and framing an idea or impres-sion; and
2. the divisions between paragraphs aren't random but indicate a shift in focus.

DEVELOP YOUR IDEAS

You are not likely to sit down and consciously ask yourself, "What pattern shall I use to develop this paragraph?" What comes first is the idea you intend to develop; the structure of the paragraph should flow from the idea itself and the way you want to discuss or expand it.

You may take one or several paragraphs to develop an idea fully. For a definition alone, you could write one paragraph or 10, depending on the complexity of the subject and the nature of the assignment. Just remember that ideas need development and that each new paragraph signals a change in idea.

CONSIDER THE TOPIC SENTENCE

Skilled skim readers know that they can get the general drift of a book simply by reading the first sentence of each paragraph. The reason is that most paragraphs begin by stating the central idea to be developed. If you are writing your essay from a formal plan, you will probably find that each section and subsection will generate the topic sentence for a new paragraph.

Like the thesis statement for the essay as a whole, the topic sentence is not obligatory. In some paragraphs the controlling idea is not stated until the middle or even the end, and in others it is not stated at all but merely implied. Nevertheless, it's a good idea to think of a topic sentence for every paragraph. That way you'll be sure that each one has a readily graspable point and is clearly connected to what comes before and after. When revising your initial draft, check to see that each paragraph is held together by a topic sentence, either stated or implied. If you find that you can't formulate one, you should probably rework the whole paragraph.

MAINTAIN FOCUS

A clear paragraph should contain only those details that are in some way related to the central idea. It should also be structured so that the details are easily seen to be related. One way of showing these relationships is to keep the same grammatical subject in most of the sentences that make up the paragraph. When the grammatical subject keeps shifting, a paragraph loses focus, as in the following example (see Cluett & Ahlborn, 1965, p. 51):

> **orig.** Students play a variety of sports these days. In the fall, football and field hockey still attract many, although an increasing number now play soccer. For some, basketball is the favourite when the fall season is over, but you will find that swimming, volleyball, and gymnastics are also popular. Cold winter temperatures bring hockey, skating, and skiing. In spring, students take up soccer again, while track and field, baseball, and tennis also attract many participants.

Here the grammatical subject (underlined) changes from sentence to sentence. Notice how much stronger the focus becomes when all the sentences have the same grammatical subject—either the same noun, a synonym, or a related pronoun:

> **rev.** Students play a variety of sports these days. In the fall, many still choose football and field hockey, although an increasing number now

play soccer. When the fall season is over, some turn to basketball; others prefer swimming, volleyball, or gymnastics. In cold winter temperatures many students enjoy hockey, skating, and skiing. In spring, some take up soccer again, while others choose track and field, baseball, or tennis.

Naturally it's not always possible to retain the same grammatical subject throughout a paragraph. If you were comparing the athletic pursuits of boys and girls, for example, you would have to switch back and forth between boys and girls as your grammatical subject. In the same way, you have to shift when you are discussing examples of an idea or exceptions to it.

AVOID MONOTONY

If most or all of the sentences in your paragraph have the same grammatical subject, how do you avoid boring your reader? There are two easy ways:

1. **Use substitute words.** Pronouns, either personal (*I, we, you, he, she, it, they*) or demonstrative (*this, that, those*), can replace the subject, as can synonyms. The revised paragraph on student athletics, for example, uses the pronouns *some, many,* and *others* as substitutes for *students.* Most well-written paragraphs have a liberal sprinkling of these substitute words. However, you must ensure that the pronoun refers to the correct subject. The relationship between pronoun and noun cannot be left for the reader to decipher.
2. **"Bury" the subject by putting something in front of it.** When the subject is placed in the middle of the sentence rather than at the beginning, it's less obvious to the reader. If you take another look at the revised paragraph, you'll see that in several sentences there is a word or phrase in front of the subject. Even a single word, such as *first, then, lately,* or *moreover,* will do the trick.

LINK YOUR IDEAS

To create coherent paragraphs, you need to link your ideas clearly. Linking words and expressions are those connectors—conjunctions and conjunctive adverbs—that show the relationship between one sentence, or part of a sentence, and another. They're also known as transition words and phrases because they form a bridge from one thought to another.

Make a habit of using linking words when you shift from one grammatical subject or idea to the next, whether the shift occurs within a single paragraph or as you move from one paragraph to another. The following are some of the most common connectors and the logical relations they indicate:

Linking word	Logical relation
again also and furthermore in addition likewise moreover similarly	addition to previous idea
alternatively although but by contrast despite, in spite of even so however nevertheless on the other hand rather yet	change from previous idea
accordingly as a result consequently for this reason hence so therefore thus	summary or conclusion

Numerical terms such as *first*, *second*, and *third* also work well as links.

VARY PARAGRAPH LENGTH BUT AVOID EXTREMES
Ideally, academic writing will have a balance of long and short paragraphs. However, it's best to avoid the extremes—especially the one-sentence

paragraph, which can only state an idea without explaining or developing it. A series of very short paragraphs is usually a sign that you have not developed your ideas in enough detail or that you have started new paragraphs unnecessarily. On the other hand, a succession of long paragraphs can be difficult to read. In deciding when to start a new paragraph, consider what is clearest and most helpful for the reader.

A few general considerations regarding paragraph lengths include the following:

- A paragraph should consist of at least two sentences dealing with the topic or idea introduced in the opening sentence.
- Don't end a paragraph with a sentence that directly introduces the reader to what follows (e.g., "In the next paragraph, I will discuss homework regulations.").
- Paragraphs should not exceed a page of text. If long paragraphs are necessary for your voice or orientation, insert quotations to offer the reader a respite.

BE CONCISE

At one time or another, you will probably be tempted to pad your writing. Whatever the reason—you need to write 2,000 or 3,000 words and have enough to say for only 1,000, or you think length is strength and hope to get a better mark for the extra words—padding is a mistake.

Strong writing is always concise yet, at the same time, provides enough detail and supporting information to carry the main thesis. It leaves out anything that does not serve some communicative or stylistic purpose, and it says as much as possible in as few words as possible. Concise writing will help you do better on both your essays and your exams.

Use Adverbs and Adjectives Sparingly

Don't sprinkle adverbs and adjectives everywhere, and don't use combinations of modifiers unless you are sure they clarify your meaning. One well-chosen word is always better than a series of synonyms:

orig. As well as being <u>costly</u> and <u>financially extravagant</u>, the venture is <u>reckless</u> and <u>risky</u>.

rev. The venture is <u>risky</u> as well as <u>costly</u>.

Avoid Noun Clusters

A recent trend in some writing is to use nouns as adjectives (as in the phrase *noun cluster*). This device can be effective occasionally, but frequent use can produce a monstrous pile of nouns. Breaking up noun clusters may not always result in fewer words, but it will make your writing easier to read:

orig.   insurance plan revision summary

rev.   summary of the revised insurance plan

Avoid Chains of Relative Clauses

Sentences full of clauses beginning with *which*, *that*, or *who* are usually wordier than necessary. Try reducing some of those clauses to phrases or single words:

orig.   The solutions that were discussed last night have a practical benefit, which is easily grasped by people who have no technical training.

rev.   The solutions discussed last night have a practical benefit, easily grasped by non-technical people.

Try Reducing Clauses to Phrases or Words

Independent clauses can often be reduced by subordination. Here are a few examples:

orig.   The report was written in a clear and concise manner, and it was widely read.

rev.   Written in a clear and concise manner, the report was widely read.

rev.   Clear and concise, the report was widely read.

orig.   His plan was of a radical nature and was a source of embarrassment to his employer.

rev.   His radical plan embarrassed his employer.

Eliminate Clichés and Circumlocutions

Trite or roundabout phrases may flow from your pen automatically, but they make for stale prose. Unnecessary words are deadwood; be prepared to slash ruthlessly to keep your writing vital:

Wordy	Revised
at this point in time	now
consensus of opinion	consensus
due to the fact that	because
in all likelihood	likely
in all probability	probably
in the eventuality that	if
in the near future	soon
it could be said that	possibly, maybe
when all is said and done	[omit]

Avoid *It is* and *There is* Beginnings

Although it may not always be possible, try to avoid beginning sentences with *It is* or *There is (are)*. Your sentences will be crisper and more concise:

orig. There is little time remaining for the sales manager to reverse the financial trend.

rev. Little time remains for the sales manager to reverse the financial trend.

BE FORCEFUL

Developing a forceful, vigorous style simply means learning some common tricks of the trade and practising them until they become habit.

Choose Active over Passive Verbs

An active verb creates more energy than a passive one does:

Active: She threw the ball.

Passive: The ball was thrown by her.

Moreover, passive constructions tend to produce awkward, convoluted phrasing. Writers of bureaucratic documents are among the worst offenders:

It has been decided that the utilization of small rivers in the province for purposes of generating hydroelectric power should be studied by our department and that a report to the deputy <u>should be made</u> by our director as soon as possible.

The passive verbs in this mouthful make it hard to tell who is doing what. Passive verbs are appropriate in four cases:

1. When the subject is the passive recipient of some action:

   The cabinet minister <u>was heckled</u> by the angry crowd.

2. When you want to emphasize the object rather than the person acting:

   The antipollution devices in all three plants <u>will be improved</u>.

3. When you want to avoid an awkward shift from one subject to another in a sentence or paragraph:

   The Jesuits began to convert the Hurons but <u>were attacked by</u> the Iroquois band before they had completed the mission.

4. When you want to avoid placing responsibility or blame:

   Several errors <u>were made</u> in the calculations.

When these exceptions don't apply, make an effort to use active verbs for a livelier style.

Use Personal Subjects

Most of us find it more interesting to learn about people than about things. Wherever possible, therefore, make the subjects of your sentences personal. This trick goes hand in hand with the use of active verbs. Almost any sentence becomes livelier with active verbs and a personal subject:

orig. The <u>outcome</u> of the union members' vote <u>was</u> the <u>decision</u> to resume work on Monday.

rev. The <u>union members voted</u> to return to work on Monday.

Here's another example:

orig.   It can be assumed that an agreement was reached, since there were smiles on both management and union sides when the meeting was concluded.

rev.   We can assume that management and the union reached an agreement, since both sides were smiling when they concluded the meeting.

(or)

rev.   Apparently management and the union reached an agreement, since both sides were smiling when they concluded the meeting.

Use Concrete Details

Concrete details are easier to understand—and to remember—than abstract theories. Whenever you are discussing abstract concepts, always provide specific examples and illustrations. If you have a choice between a concrete word and an abstract one, choose the concrete. Consider this sentence:

The French explored the northern territory and traded with the Indigenous peoples.

Now see how a few specific details can bring the facts to life:

The French voyageurs paddled their way along the river systems of the North, trading their blankets and copper kettles with the Indigenous peoples for furs.

Adding concrete details doesn't mean getting rid of all abstractions. Just try to find the proper balance. The above example is one instance where adding words, if they are concrete and correct, can improve your writing.

Make Important Ideas Stand Out

Experienced writers know how to manipulate sentences in order to emphasize certain points. The following are some of their techniques.

PLACE KEY WORDS IN STRATEGIC POSITIONS

The positions of emphasis in a sentence are the beginning and, above all, the end. If you want to bring your point home with force, don't put the key words in the middle of the sentence. Save them for the end:

> **orig.** People are less afraid of losing wealth than of losing face in this image-conscious society.

> **rev.** In this image-conscious society, people are less afraid of losing wealth than of losing face.

SUBORDINATE MINOR IDEAS

Small children connect incidents with a string of *ands*, as if everything were of equal importance:

> Our bus was delayed, and we were late for school, and we missed the test.

As they grow up, however, they learn to subordinate—that is, to make one part of a sentence less important in order to emphasize another point:

> Because the bus was delayed, we were late and missed the test.

Major ideas stand out more and connections become clearer when minor ideas are subordinated:

> **orig.** Night came and the ship slipped away from her captors.

> **rev.** When night came, the ship slipped away from her captors.

Make your most important idea the subject of the main clause, and try to put it at the end, where it will be most emphatic:

> **orig.** I was relieved when I saw my marks.

> **rev.** When I saw my marks, I was relieved.

VARY SENTENCE STRUCTURE

As with anything else, variety adds spice to writing. One way of adding variety that will also make an important idea stand out is to use a periodic rather than a simple sentence structure.

Most sentences follow the simple pattern of subject–verb–object (plus modifiers):

The <u>premier</u> <u>lost</u> the <u>election</u>.
     s   **v**   **o**

A *simple sentence* such as this one gives the main idea at the beginning and therefore creates little tension. A *periodic sentence*, on the other hand, does not give the main clause until the end, after one or more subordinate clauses:

Since the premier had failed to keep her promises or to inspire the voters, in the next election <u>she</u> <u>was defeated</u>.
            s   **v**

The longer the periodic sentence, the greater the suspense and the more emphatic the final part. Since this high-tension structure is more difficult to read than the simple sentence, your reader would be exhausted if you used it too often. Save it for those times when you want to make a very strong point.

VARY SENTENCE LENGTH

A short sentence can add impact to an important point, especially when it comes after a series of longer sentences. This technique can be particularly useful for conclusions. Don't overdo it, though—a string of long sentences may be monotonous, but a string of short ones can make your writing sound like a children's book.

Still, academic papers usually have too many long sentences rather than too many short ones. Since short sentences are easier to read, try breaking up clusters of long ones. Check any sentence of more than 20 words or so to see if it will benefit from being split.

USE CONTRAST

Just as a jeweller highlights a diamond by displaying it against dark velvet, you can highlight an idea by placing it against a contrasting background:

orig.   Most employees in industry do not have indexed pensions.

rev.   <u>Unlike civil servants</u>, most employees in industry do not have indexed pensions.

Using parallel phrasing will increase the effect of the contrast:

> Although <u>she often spoke</u> to business groups, <u>she seldom spoke</u> in Parliament.

USE A WELL-PLACED ADVERB OR CORRELATIVE CONSTRUCTION
Adding an adverb or two can sometimes help you dramatize a concept:

orig. Although I dislike the proposal, I must accept it as the practical answer.

rev. Although <u>emotionally</u> I dislike the concept, <u>intellectually</u> I must accept it as the practical answer.

Correlatives such as *both . . . and* or *not only . . . but also* can be used to emphasize combinations as well:

orig. Professor Nderu was a good instructor and a good friend.

rev. Professor Nderu was <u>both</u> a good instructor <u>and</u> a good friend.

(or)

rev. Professor Nderu was <u>not only</u> a good instructor <u>but also</u> a good friend.

USE REPETITION
Repetition is a highly effective device for adding emphasis:

> <u>He fought</u> injustice and corruption. <u>He fought</u> complacent politicians and inept policies. <u>He fought</u> hard, but he always <u>fought</u> fairly.

Of course, you would use such a dramatic technique only on rare occasions.

SOME FINAL ADVICE

Write before You Revise
No one expects you to sit down and put all this information into practice as soon as you start to write. You would feel so constrained that it would be hard to get anything down on paper at all. You will be better off if you begin concentrating on these guidelines during the final stages of the writing process, when you are looking critically at what you have already written. Some

experienced writers can combine the creative and critical functions, but most of us find it easier to write a rough draft first before starting the detailed task of revising and editing.

Writing can be difficult, and there is no question that the many and required revisions can become daunting. However, English is an evolving and subtle language that lends itself to interesting twists and turns. Within reason, always try to have some fun with your writing. Over time, you will develop a unique writing style and the process will become easier.

Use Your Ears

Your ears are probably your best critics; make good use of them. Before producing a final copy of any piece of writing, read it out loud in a clear voice. The difference between cumbersome and fluent passages will be unmistakable.

REFERENCES

Cluett, R., & Ahlborn, L. (1965). *Effective English prose: Writing for meaning, reading for style*. New York, NY: L. W. Singer.

CHAPTER 8

Creating an Education Portfolio and Writing a Professional Journal

OBJECTIVES

- To appreciate the purpose of an education portfolio
- To begin the process of portfolio creation and long-term maintenance
- To view journal writing as a form of professional self-reflection
- To begin writing for a wider academic audience

INTRODUCTION

The education portfolio and professional journal are two emerging trends in education that can benefit professional development. Although portfolios have been part of the field for only 30 years, they have quickly become a major element in teacher evaluation and professional self-reflection. Journal writing has a slightly longer history, but has not created the same level of enthusiasm. Nonetheless, these complimentary forms are powerful tools for individual teachers, who can use them to ponder how their own experiences and knowledge can be shared with a wider professional audience. Ongoing debate and critical investigation of issues keeps any body of knowledge open and relevant. Therefore, all educators must also embrace broader communication as a vital component of their working lives.

THE EDUCATION PORTFOLIO

For centuries, artists created portfolios of their work to show to prospective patrons. Today, architects, designers, and writers have portfolios that contain examples of their current ideas and past works. An education portfolio allows a teacher to review and reflect on his or her performance and accomplishments. It is also a means to provide information to the school board or other administrative body during external evaluations. Therefore, the use of education portfolios has increased in popularity and become ingrained in the general psyche of new teachers. A growing number of school boards, ministries and faculties of education, and other certification organizations now require a portfolio for graduation or certification purposes.

A professional portfolio has merit only if its individual components are identifiable, easily retrievable, maintained regularly, evaluated periodically, and shared with colleagues. A file drawer of assorted letters, memos, pictures, student projects, and parent letters is insufficient. Instead, your education portfolio must contain a collection of carefully selected items that, in their totality, represent significant points in your role as an educator. This compilation may include a wide variety of papers and objects, such as the following:

- annotated bibliographies
- awards
- classroom management schemes
- conference summaries
- credentials, licences, and authorizations
- curriculum initiatives
- curriculum vitae (CV) and resumé
- essays and research papers
- field trip photos and comments
- lesson plans
- formal appreciation letters and other acknowledgements
- newspaper articles/letters to the editor
- notes from students, parents, etc.
- peer/collegial evaluations
- photographs, pictures, and drawings
- professional association memberships
- student learning contracts
- transcripts and academic records

Portfolios and Confidentiality

When selecting material for your portfolio, you must respect and protect the privacy of others. Remember, your portfolio has to be seen by others if its function of external evaluation and reflection is to be fully engaged. While you are free to include items developed by you or regarding you, you must be very careful with anything that identifies a child or a parent. Generally speaking, do not include pictures of students or parents without first getting their written permission and do not give a student's or parent's contact information. Never enclose any personal letters/official reports detailing a student's physical, academic or emotional health.

Portfolio Assembly

Unlike a research paper, a portfolio is always a work-in-progress. As you, the teacher, are constantly changing and growing, so too will your portfolio. That said, your portfolio should not be so unwieldy or chaotic that it cannot serve any purpose.

In most cases, the basic portfolio is kept in a three-ring binder and contains many sections with a concise table of contents. Another option is an electronic portfolio. You could, for example, create DVDs of your portfolio and distribute them as required. In some cases, your portfolio might be a personalized website with restricted, time-limited access. In this way, you can authorize others to view your portfolio but still maintain control. Whatever format you select (and you may use multiple types to meet varying needs), you are the creator, editor, and marshal of the material.

Along with your basic portfolio, you may also have a secondary set of materials. Because you cannot constantly update your portfolio, this collection can be reviewed on a regular basis (perhaps twice a year) and its components validated for inclusion in the basic portfolio. As you add new material, you may discard items that are no longer relevant or representative of your experience. Just because something has been included in the portfolio does not mean that it is a permanent feature. In many ways, an education portfolio is a living unit and must never be allowed to become static.

Although education portfolios are relatively new, there are two methods concerning their contents: the Interstate Teacher Assessment and Support Consortium (InTASC) and the university. These styles each have guidelines that can help you assemble your portfolio.

The InTASC Guidelines

InTASC was formed in the early 1990s by American educators who were concerned about teacher training and evaluation. While InTASC is not an official government group and has no authority over school boards or ministries, its guidelines for teacher training have received wide support from educational stakeholders throughout Canada and the United States. Using these principles as a professional baseline, ministries and faculties of education are adjusting the points to reflect local needs and issues.

InTASC presents 10 standards, which are organized into broader categories and cover all facets of the education process:

1. **The Learner and Learning**

   Standard #1: Learner Development
   The teacher understands how learners grow and develop, recognizing that patterns of learning and development vary individually within and across the cognitive, linguistic, social, emotional, and physical areas, and designs and implements developmentally appropriate and challenging learning experiences.

   Standard #2: Learning Differences
   The teacher uses understanding of individual differences and diverse cultures and communities to ensure inclusive learning environments that enable each learner to meet high standards.

   Standard #3: Learning Environments
   The teacher works with others to create environments that support individual and collaborative learning, and that encourage positive social interaction, active engagement in learning, and self-motivation.

2. **Content**

   Standard #4: Content Knowledge
   The teacher understands the central concepts, tools of inquiry, and structures of the discipline(s) he or she teaches and creates learning experiences that make the discipline accessible and meaningful for learners to assure mastery of the content.

   Standard #5: Application of Content
   The teacher understands how to connect concepts and use differing perspectives to engage learners in critical thinking, creativity, and collaborative problem solving related to authentic local and global issues.

3. **Instructional Practice**

   Standard #6: Assessment
   The teacher understands and uses multiple methods of assessment to engage learners in their own growth, to monitor learner progress, and to guide the teacher's and learner's decision-making.

Standard #7: Planning for Instruction
The teacher plans instruction that supports every student in meeting rigorous learning goals by drawing upon knowledge of content areas, curriculum, cross-disciplinary skills, and pedagogy, as well as knowledge of learners and the community context.

Standard #8: Instructional Strategies
The teacher understands and uses a variety of instructional strategies to encourage learners to develop deep understanding of content areas and their connections, and to build skills to apply knowledge in meaningful ways.

4. **Professional Responsibility**

Standard #9: Professional Learning and Ethical Practice
The teacher engages in ongoing professional learning and uses evidence to continually evaluate his or her practice, particularly the effects of his or her choices and actions on others (learners, families, other professionals, and the community), and adapts the practice to meet the learner's needs.

Standard #10: Leadership and Collaboration
The teacher seeks appropriate leadership roles and opportunities to take responsibility for student learning, to collaborate with learners, families, colleagues, and other school professionals, and community members to ensure learner growth, and to advance the profession. (Council of Chief State School Officers, 2011, pp. 8–9)

These principles can be used as a general table of contents for your portfolio. However, this structure emphasizes that your portfolio doesn't simply highlight surface issues but must allow you and others the opportunity to gauge your effectiveness as a teacher from several vantage points. While allowing room to manoeuvre, the InTASC guidelines also provide a path to follow and explore.

Using these standards as a basis for your portfolio also raises certain questions: How will you select materials and documents for each section? How will you subdivide each large area to reflect your own individual practice? Where might you need to seek deeper understanding? Are there certain areas where you could be more effective? These questions represent the kind of professional and personal self-reflection that you will experience in your role as an educator.

The InTASC list (especially Standard #9) clearly stresses the need for teachers to become more self-reflective and judgmental concerning their professional actions and educative outcomes. The days of the teacher being a simple disseminator of a forced top-down curriculum and mandated texts are long gone. While vestiges of this hierarchical system remain, teachers are generally being asked to take on more responsibility and become self-reflective practitioners within an expanding team. Educators currently have a say in textbook selection and course-scheduling concerns, sit on curriculum committees, help write local and provincial examinations, and meet with other professionals and specialists regarding a child's family and social life. In many places, they are viewed as leaders. With this added status and responsibility comes increased accountability, which the education portfolio can help assess.

THE UNIVERSITY MODEL

Over the last decade, many education faculties and other credentialing agencies have struggled to introduce the portfolio into initial teacher-training accreditation programs. This implementation is not a simple matter because there are many administrative jurisdictions involved, along with a changing political and educational landscape.

One organization that has developed portfolio guidelines is McGill University's Faculty of Education. Broadly adhering to the InTASC principles, McGill's "Portfolio & Professional Competencies" (www.mcgill.ca/ost/students/portfolio) are embedded in the 12 teaching aptitudes mandated by the Quebec Ministry of Education. As with the InTASC standards, McGill's guidelines provide an overarching framework for an education portfolio. However, this university model contains both required and optional content:

Required Content

- table of contents
- section dividers or chapters for DVDs
- CV and/or resumé
- statement of education philosophy
- professional competencies (the 12 mandated Quebec principles)
- action plan
- learning evaluation situations and individual education plans
- appreciation of community of learners

Optional Content

- suggested section headings (autobiography, professional identity, teaching and learning, embracing cultural diversity)
- letters of reference
- letters of appreciation
- photos of students in class
- photos and descriptions of special projects
- professional log entries
- extracurricular activities
- DVD of teaching
- examples of original classroom materials
- accounts of professional involvement
- evaluation forms from co-operating teachers and supervisors
- transcript from B.Ed. program (McGill University, 2011, pp. 2–3)

In this evolving university model, education students begin the development process immediately and modify their portfolio throughout the program. A "final" portfolio is both a graduation requirement and a potential employment element.

As well as providing a philosophical outline via the mandated and suggested contents, this structure also offers four self-assessment tools that students may use to monitor their portfolios (McGill, 2011):

- **Content:** provide a complete professional profile; show intellectual leadership and energy and depth of reflection and insight; use a variety of documentation that is precise, detailed, and compelling; focus on accomplishments and reflections.
- **Organization:** ensure that the material is easy to follow, well developed, and logically structured.
- **Presentation:** ensure that material is easy to read, professional, accessible, complete, and relevant to the intended audience; choose visuals that enhance content; use design features that will facilitate reading.
- **Writing:** present ideas in a coherent and cohesive manner; ensure that language is free from all mechanical and technical errors; use excellent structure; make writing concise, clear, dynamic, and engaging. (p. 4)

PROFESSIONAL JOURNALS

As part of the self-reflection process, you may want to engage in narrative writing, which recounts real education experiences. One type of narrative writing that is becoming increasingly common among teachers is the professional journal. Normally, such a journal is not meant for public consumption. It is a private place where you can openly comment on events that occur in your professional life and express your emotions. In a sense, a journal allows you to vent steam without fear of any repercussions. It is also a vehicle for reflecting on the past and pondering future possibilities.

Like the education portfolio, you may keep either an electronic or handwritten journal. Some teachers prefer the electronic mode because, if they have second thoughts, they can quickly delete what they've written. The electronic format also enables them to join ideas or entries more easily. However, the use of pen and paper is more intimate and demands greater concentration. It is also possible to print typed pages and keep them in a book or to use both formats.

Remember that your journal is not an agenda or simple list of events. Do not use your timetable as a template. Use your journal to reflect on those things that touched you in some emotional, professional, and/or personal way. While you can write in any style, an efficient way of journal writing is storytelling. Telling stories allows you to review past events and bring yourself up to date. In some cases, little may have happened in regards to a specific story; however, some incidents may have consumed your entire week. Storytelling also allows you to represent yourself and other participants as a cast of characters. You can even become a third-person narrator and relate the events more impartially.

Whatever the format or style you choose, try to write in your journal for at least half an hour once a week. Schedule a time to just sit down and write about the past week's events. The topics are endless—your thoughts can review each day in sequence, mention a particular incident with a troubled student, summarize an enjoyable conversation with a parent or colleague, or even deal with more mundane issues such as bus duty, dress codes, and the toils of homework supervision. Setting aside this time will prove most beneficial over a school year.

ACADEMIC AND PROFESSIONAL WRITING

As an educator, you not only have an obligation to reflect on your professional development but also to share with colleagues. Part of being an active and creative member of the education field is writing for a larger professional audience.

Through your various professional associations, you will receive all manner of newsletters, memos, updates, peer- and non-peer-reviewed journals, and conference information. As well as allowing you to keep up with the latest developments in your field, these print and digital items will provide possible leads for publishing your academic and professional writing. For example, most professional associations accept submissions from members and openly provide manuscript guidelines. In a sense, these associations exist to help their members publish relevant information. Further, the recent proliferation of electronic journals has opened the market for new authors.

You can begin this part of your teaching career slowly, perhaps by summarizing a conference for a newsletter or reviewing a new book for your local teachers' association. As you gain experience and confidence with these writing tasks, you can then move on to other projects, such as critiques of suggested curriculum alterations or even a paper on an in-school pilot project.

While some may eschew such professional and academic writing as too hard and philosophical or even as being unrelated to the practicalities of the classroom, this is simply not the case. All educators have something interesting to say, and we enhance the teaching profession when we share our concerns and experiences with our colleagues.

That said, it is important to remember that, while we are all protected by freedom of speech and privacy laws, educators have to be extra careful when making public statements. Your journal is private, but whatever you write in a public forum—a letter to the editor, an article in an e-journal, a post on a social networking site, etc.—is available for mass consumption. As we discussed in Chapter 4, you must be respectful even if you disagree with someone's views. You must also refrain from using hateful, derogatory, or foul language. Most importantly, you cannot espouse views that oppose those held by your employer.

REFERENCES

Council of Chief State School Officers. (2011). Interstate Teacher Assessment and Support Consortium (InTASC) model core teaching standards: A resource for state dialogue. Washington, DC: Author. Retrieved from http://www.ccsso.org/Documents/2011/InTASC_Model_Core_Teaching_Standards_2011.pdf

McGill University. (2011). Professional portfolios for B.Ed. students. Retrieved from http://www.mcgill.ca/files/ost/Portfolio_Guidelines_REVISION_March_2011.pdf

CHAPTER 9

Writing Report Cards and Other Evaluations

OBJECTIVES

- To understand the different reporting formats
- To view official report cards as legal and educational documents
- To follow the guidelines for writing report card comments

INTRODUCTION

Your current experience with reporting tools has probably been from the vantage point of the student, the recipient of the document. As an educator, you will become the creator of the report. Because these reports are extremely important and must be as accurate as possible, writing them can be a stressful task. Teachers at every level worry about filling out reports regarding a student's progress. However, understanding the various types of reporting, particularly the report card, will make this part of your job easier.

REPORTING SCHEMES

Although this chapter focuses on report cards, you will write various types of evaluations in your teaching career. Here are the characteristics of the main formats.

Issued by an authorized school or school board, a report card is an official document that details a student's academic ranking and usually includes teacher comments. Depending on legal requirements, it may also include other aspects of a student's life, such as absenteeism, tardiness, and disciplinary actions. A report card is usually printed with the school's or school board's logo or on its letterhead, using high-quality, coloured bond paper or even card stock. It may also have places for signatures (the principal's, teacher's, and parents'/legal guardians'). In most cases, a report card is completed at the end of each school term and at the end of a scholastic year. As a formal document, a report card cannot be revised once it has been issued.

A progress report is a somewhat less formal but equally official document that may be issued by the school periodically during a term. The purpose of this type of report is to indicate ongoing academic achievement based on factors that are still evolving. In other words, it focuses on general trends rather than specific examination stages. Progress reports are usually presented in a less rigid manner than report cards. For example, they may be printed on regular bond paper, with or without official logos.

Another reporting format is the transcript, which is normally a computerized statement indicating courses and grades. Rarely will a transcript contain anecdotal comments. Its main purpose is to clearly state what courses (by name and number) were taken in which term and what grades were received. In many transcripts, individual student grades are ranked by the class average as well as class averages over time. Furthermore, the student's overall standing is determined by a statistical grade point average (GPA), which is usually also ranked with others in the same class, course, or program. Official transcripts are issued by an education authority on special paper with appropriate seals. Unofficial transcripts (on cheaper paper without seals) are also available for verification and student use.

The fourth type of report, the checklist, is an informal way of quickly notifying parents of their children's academic standing. The list is provided by the school or school board and includes tasks, competencies, and/or operations under broad headings. In most checklists, a teacher simply indicates which items have been successfully completed. Checklists are frequently used in sports, industrial arts classes, and other specific task-orientated endeavours.

Finally, the report letter/memo is another way for schools to inform parents about their children. This format is open in structure and is most commonly used to contact parents regarding non-academic issues, such as discipline problems, team work, sports concerns, and medical issues. A letter or memo is written on the school's official letterhead and printed on quality bond paper.

CONTEXT AND EMOTIONS

Whatever its type, an evaluation is a snapshot of a particular time and context. As such, the report or individual grade may have different meanings.

For example, what does receiving 80 per cent on a test mean in terms of your academic standing? If everyone else received 65 per cent or less, your grade is impressive. If only three other people wrote the exam, however, your competition was a tad sparse. Likewise, a grade of 80 per cent on an exam developed and graded by your teacher and taken by only one class cannot be compared to the same grade obtained on a national test scored by outside evaluators and written by hundreds of students. A host of other possibilities (Was group work permitted? Could dictionaries be consulted? Was the project completed in school or at home?) will also affect the meaning of the report or grade.

Another factor to consider is the objectivity of the marker. It is clearly recognized in educational circles that the more removed a classroom teacher is from the evaluation process, the more impartial the evaluation. For example, would knowing that a student is overweight, struggling in his other classes, and trying to cope with his parents' divorce lead you to overlook the disorganization, sloppiness, and poor spelling in his final project?

Consider another example. A colleague writes, administers, and grades the mathematics examination for your class. Unfortunately, over one-third of the students fail the test. Does this result mean that you are a poor teacher? Was the test too difficult or the time allotted insufficient?

Reporting is not an exact science. Context and emotions can play a role; however, solid pedagogical reporting requires that, whatever the situation or your emotional stake in it, you must be objective.

REPORT CARDS

Report Card Categories

Report cards are usually pre-printed and generic, allowing them to be used by many people over long periods of time. Although school boards leave room for unique local situations, most group reporting into several broad categories:

- preschool to kindergarten
- elementary school (grades 1 to 5)
- middle school (grades 6 to 9)
- secondary school (grades 10 to 12)

In the first two groups, students usually have only a few teachers. Therefore, it is commonly the homeroom or main teacher who completes the report card.

If specialist educators (e.g., physical education or second language teachers) must provide marks or comments, they give this information to the teacher compiling the report card. In some cases, report cards will "make the rounds," with each teacher recording the relevant grade and comments.

In these groups, it is also common for percentages to be replaced with letter grades (A, B, C, etc.) or descriptions (satisfactory, making improvement, needs improvement, unsatisfactory, etc.). The report card will usually include space for anecdotal comments. Some designs allow the comments to be typed into the allotted space; others require that they be handwritten.

Because students in the latter categories often have multiple teachers, passing reports around or assigning the task to one teacher is impractical. Therefore, report cards at the middle and secondary levels are often electronic, with individual subject teachers entering grades and comments into a centralized database. Grades at these levels are also more precise, using percentages or a detailed letter ranking (A+, A, A–, etc.).

Generally speaking, attachments are not permitted in any report card. This form of evaluation is designed to be a separate entity, and there are usually no convenient ways to add further reports or explanatory material securely.

Student Input

The report card is a legal document designed to inform parents, but it is evolving into a document that also informs students. In a growing number of cases, students are asked to read the report card, talk to their teacher(s) about work habits and aspirations, recommend personal improvement strategies, and, in some cases, sign the document. This shift to a child–parent dyad is becoming particularly common at the middle and secondary school levels, where individual students are asked to take a responsible and proactive approach to learning. In these situations, it is necessary to write for both parent and student understanding.

WRITING REPORT CARD COMMENTS

Part of your responsibility as a teacher will be to explain educational issues to parents and ensure that both parents and students understand the situation. One way to do so is to write concise, focused, and authoritative report card comments. Even though it is incumbent upon each teacher to develop his or her own style that suits the subjects taught and the ages of the students, there are some general considerations:

- Write in simple, rather than complex or compound, sentences.

    ✓ Imogen fails to complete her homework most of the time.

    ✓ Roberto's math skills are improving.

- Use active verbs.

    ✓ Pierre daydreams and drifts off task every day.

    ✓ Diana focuses and works intently on individual projects.

- Do not use transitional words or phrases.
- Write in the simple present or past tense, not future tense.
- Avoid vague statements.

    ✗ Judith is a pleasure to have in my class.

    ✗ I wish all my students were as attentive as Samir.

- Do not use professional jargon or technical language; use terms that parents and students will understand.
- Never make disparaging comments.

    ✗ Katya should worry more about her reading and less about her looks.

    ✗ Julio is a busybody.

- Use legible and neat penmanship when writing comments by hand.

Writing effective report card comments is a unique skill. Mastering it will allow parents and students to understand the evaluation. Communication between you, your students, and their parents will become easier and more productive. Parental co-operation and student involvement may also improve.

CHAPTER 10

Writing a Curriculum Vitae, Resumé, and Cover Letter

OBJECTIVES

- To construct and maintain a curriculum vitae, resumé, and cover letter
- To customize these documents for particular job opportunities
- To learn guidelines for completing application forms and submitting e-mail applications
- To consider privacy issues when applying for a job

INTRODUCTION

Whether you are seeking a teaching position, promotion, or tenure, you will eventually need to write a curriculum vitae, resumé, and cover letter. This chapter will look at the components of and writing guidelines for each type, as well as other forms of application. We will also look at the issue of confidentiality when submitting any application, especially electronically.

CURRICULUM VITAE

The Latin word *vitae* is commonly translated as "a brief biography" or "a short account of life." A curriculum vitae (commonly referred to as a CV, cv, or Vitae), then, is a brief account of your education and experience. A CV is usually required in academic realms when applying for teaching, research, academic, and/or general educational positions.

Although there are no hard and fast requirements regarding length, and some CVs can grow quite long over time, you must ensure that your CV remains precise and organized. There are also standards regarding content. For example, information is presented in reverse chronological order so that readers see the most recent item first. A CV is devoid of personal narrative, pictures, and attachments. Any supporting documentation is provided in an education portfolio (see Chapter 8). CV sections can be changed, rearranged, and renamed as the need arises, but the document should include the following general categories:

- **Personal information.**   Give your legal name (centred at the top of the page and in bold and/or capital letters), full address (with postal code), and telephone number. Also include any other contact information (cellphone number, fax number, e-mail address, personal websites) that you want the organization to have access to and/or use.

- **Formal education.**   This section lists the educational institutions you've attended, the years you studied there, the programs you took, and the degrees, certificates, and/or diplomas you obtained. Even if you didn't finish or if you failed a certain program, you must still include it so that the educational timeline is respected. You must also indicate that you did not complete the program. You can give your reasons for leaving at the interview, if the issue is raised.

  When compiling your education history, remember that most employers won't view your elementary school experiences as relevant or indicative of your current potential as an employee. Secondary school may still be relevant, especially at the beginning of your career.

  Be very careful when supplying your education information—it will be checked by your prospective employer and verified by the official documents that you will have to provide later. Fudging information is never a good thing to do on a CV or any other type of professional document. Falsification, no matter how minor it may seem, can be used as immediate grounds for the withdrawal of any employment offer or for dismissal from the position, even years later.

- **Informal education.**   Your informal education should also be noted, within reason. For example, did you attend a one-week leadership conference, a non-credit workshop from your local college, or photography courses at the community centre? Include the name of the institution, the time frame, and an indication of what you studied.

- **Credentials and licences.** Clearly indicate any credentials you've received from a governmental or other certifying organization. If you are currently involved in an accreditation process, list what you plan to receive and indicate "approval pending." You can also include any licences that have lapsed (a substitute teacher's card or a temporary permit to teach one class at a high school)—just be sure to note the end date.

    You may also have credentials in related areas (certified referee for a specific event, master bridge instructor, accredited driving instructor). Although not immediately germane, they are important indicators that you have successfully completed other forms of recognized study and been granted the appropriate licences. However, listing more mundane permits, such as a driver's licence, is not appropriate in this type of document. Some educational positions may require unique credentials (a bronze medal for a swimming instructor, Red Cross first-aid certification for a physical education teacher), but they are not the norm.

- **Languages.** The ability to speak more than one language is a definite asset. Even if you aren't fluent in a particular language, state your level. For example, you could indicate your French skills by using the following qualifiers: speaking/hearing = excellent, reading = functional, writing = poor. Remember, English is also a language and must be included in the list.

    To some, computer languages and mathematics are unique languages. If you have skills in these or other areas, such as sign language or shorthand, include them in this section.

- **Work history.** Depending on your situation, this section can be divided into subcategories, such as education experience, non-education experience, summer experience, and/or student teaching experience. If you are embarking on a second career, you must include your previous employment. However, don't overload the section with every minor part-time and/or short-term job that you've ever had. Focus on jobs related to education in the broad sense: tutoring, after-school programs, theatre school, etc.

    Your in-school practicum experience can be placed in a separate section, but it would also be relevant here. Don't give the names of co-operating/assisting teachers or university supervisors; simply note the name of the school, duration, grade and/or subject levels, and responsibilities. Be clear about the kind of practicum. For example, if you did a 10-day observation, don't say that it was a 10-day student teaching experience.

- **Academic publications and presentations.** As a beginning teacher, you may not have items for this section. However, if you have, for example, made presentations at a workshop, participated at a graduate student conference, or contributed to the local newspaper, these activities need to be included in your CV.

- **Committee work and research.** Again, this section may not be appropriate for a novice teacher. The intent of this section is to highlight any research projects that you were involved in through course work and/or as a participant.

- **Awards and honours.** Any awards (scholastic, sport, academic, humanitarian, etc.) must be noted. Certificates of excellence, notices of involvement, and other forms of recognition speak well of your individual efforts. Clearly, any academic honour, such as a place on the Dean's List or a scholarship, is to be included.

- **Academic and professional associations.** This part of the CV is often overlooked. As an educator, you will belong to and support associations at all levels. For example, you might belong to the local reading association, the county historical club, or an educational honour society. This section, then, would be an alpha list of the academic and professional associations to which you are currently a member.

- **Volunteerism and community interests.** These activities are also an often neglected element of the CV. However, it is well understood that teachers who have wide community involvement and major interests outside of school and who take a positive role in their larger communities bring a great deal to the educational landscape. Therefore, your work with projects such as the local parks clean-up program, the weekly volunteer reading at the children's hospital, and non-profit fundraising should be included.

- **References.** Your list of references will change as you gain experience and training. For example, your high-school basketball coach would have been a fine reference to support your university application, but he is too far removed to be a good reference when you apply for your first teaching position. In this case, you would look to your instructors and/or co-operating/assisting teachers for references.

You might prefer to provide references only if you are asked for them. This practice is acceptable, provided that you have a list available. A reference list should include the names and professional titles of your references, along with their current contact information. Always ask permission to use a person as a reference before giving these details to anyone.

- **Varia.** This last category is a catch-all section. Did you take a six-month world cruise that makes you a better educator? Have you had an experience that makes you more empathetic to students at risk? Use this part of your CV for those incidents that may not fit into the other categories.

The CV is a document that you will update and revise regularly. As you successfully encounter another student teaching experience, complete additional university work, direct a school production, or take several workshops on various subjects, make sure that your CV accurately reflects these new experiences.

RESUMÉ

A resumé is a much shorter version of the CV and provides a snapshot of your education, accomplishments, and experience. Both forms use reverse chronological order, are precise and regularly updated, and even contain some of the same information. These similarities lead many people and organizations to use the words *CV* and *resumé* interchangeably. However, they are different documents. You must, therefore, be certain which one is required.

Think of a resumé as more than just a summary of the CV; think of it as a marketing strategy tailored to specific employers. You will still need to supply some basic information, but how you organize it and which details you emphasize are up to you. For example, your resumé for a job as a summer camp director would be different from one for a teaching position, even though both would include many of the same details.

As with your CV, your goal is to keep the resumé as concise as possible while including all the specific information that will help you "sell" yourself. A reader will lose interest in a resumé that goes on and on. On the other hand, experience or skills that seem irrelevant to you may, in fact, demonstrate an important attribute or qualification, such as a sense of responsibility or willingness to work hard.

The tone of a resumé should be upbeat, so don't draw attention to any potential weaknesses you may have, such as lack of experience in a particular area. Never list a category and then write "None"—you don't want to suggest that you lack something. Remember to adjust your list of special skills to fit each job you apply for so that the reader will see at a glance that you meet the job requirements. Finally, just as with the CV, never claim more than is true.

Here is a list of common resumé components, along with some suggestions on how to present it. Figure 10.1 represents a sample one-page resume for a beginning teacher.

- **Name.** Your name is typically placed in bold and/or in capital letters and centred at the top of the page.
- **Contact information.** This part includes your mailing address with postal code, phone and fax numbers, websites, and e-mail address. If you have a temporary student address, remember to indicate where you can be reached at other times.
- **Education.** Include any degrees, diplomas, or certificates, along with the institutions that granted them and the dates. If it will help your case and if you are short of other qualifications, you may also list courses you have taken that are relevant to the job.
- **Awards or honours.** These items may be in a separate section or included with your education details.
- **Work experience.** Give the name and location of your employers, along with your job titles and the dates of employment. Instead of outlining your duties, list your accomplishments on the job, using point form and action verbs. You can include your student teaching and practicum experience here or in a separate section.
- **Research experience or specialized skills.** This is a chance to list information that may give you an advantage in a competitive market, such as experience with certain computer programs or knowledge of a second language. If you have worked as a research assistant, be sure to state the type of work you did and the name of your employer, for example:

  > Assisted Professor Rachel Kwon with a school-based curriculum project on gender differences in academic achievement in grade 3 mathematics, Carleton University, Summer 2012.

- **Other interests** (optional). Including a few interests or achievements, such as travel or athletic or musical accomplishments, will show that you are well rounded or especially disciplined; however, avoid a long list of items that merely show passive or minimal involvement. Depending on the employer, the position you are seeking, and the amount of information you have already included in your resumé, you may choose to omit this section.
- **References.** Follow the guidelines for references in CVs.

SHELLEY MARGARET BOSPEROUS

1245 Main Street, #25 • Anytown, NL A6D 3Y7
Home: 709-123-9876 • Cell: 709-321-6789 • smb2@localmail.ca

Education:

2011–2012	Bachelor of Education (Elementary Option) Instructional University Degree: Pending
2007–2011	Bachelor of Arts (English Literature) Instructional University Degree: BA granted June 2011
2003–2007	Anytown Secondary School Diploma: Granted June 2007

Awards:

2010	Senior Class Poetry Prize, Instructional University
2009	Dean's List, Instructional University
2007	Silver Medal, Eastern Institute of Music Examinations
2005	First Prize, Piano Solo, Newfoundland Music Festival

Memberships:

2011	Instructional University Education Society (Council Member)
2009–2012	Brooke County Theatre (Actor and Director)
2008–2010	Instructional University Dramatic Society
2005–2006	Anytown Secondary School Jazz Club

School Experience:

2010–2011	Forty (40) days field work: 10 days at Springview Elementary (observation) 10 days at Oceanview Elementary (50% teaching) 10 days at Mountainview Elementary (75% teaching) 10 days at Oceanview Elementary (100% teaching)
2007–2009	Twenty-five (25) days in-school reading workshop participant Instructional University community outreach program
2006–2007	Fifteen (15) days mentoring at Springview Elementary Anytown Secondary School community program

Figure 10.1   Sample Resumé

Work Experience:
2007–2010   Nighway Hardware
                      Stock person and inventory control
                      Part-time/weekends/summers

Languages:
English: Excellent in all facets
French: Excellent speaking; functional reading and writing
Spanish: Functional speaking

References: Available upon request

Figure 10.1   Sample Resumé *(continued)*

Along with the content, the presentation of your resumé is also important. Keep the following points in mind when formatting your resumé. (These instructions—except for the first two—also apply to formatting a CV.)

- A resumé should be no longer than two pages.
- Print on only one side of the paper.
- Include your name in the header of the second page, in case the pages get separated.
- Use good-quality bond paper and eschew colours or papers with backgrounds.
- Staple the pages of your resumé in the upper left corner; do not use clips.
- Format the pages so that you do not have a full first page and an almost blank second page.
- Ensure that your resumé is free of spelling and grammatical errors.
- Use a standard font type (Times New Roman) and size (12), and use boldface for headings and subheadings only.
- When possible, print your resumé on a laser printer to ensure the best quality.

COVER LETTER

A cover letter is a succinct formal letter (see Chapter 13) that accompanies your CV or resumé. This letter indicates the recipient of your application and where you saw the job posting. It also simply states your interest in the position and asks that you be considered for the job.

You should not use the same generic letter for all applications; instead, you should craft each one to focus directly on the particular job and company in question so as to catch the attention of each particular reader. The key to any cover letter and accompanying CV or resumé is to link your skills to the position, not just state information. What matters is not what you want but what the employer needs.

One challenge in writing a cover letter is to tell your reader about yourself and your qualifications without seeming egotistical. Three tips can help:

1. Limit the number of sentences beginning with *I*. Instead, try burying *I* in the middle of some sentences, where it will be less noticeable ("For two months last summer, I worked as a . . .").
2. Avoid making unsupported, subjective claims as much as possible. Rather than saying "I have excellent research skills," you might say, "Based on my previous work, Professor Kimiko Sunahara selected me from 10 applicants to help with her in-school research project."
3. The cover letter is your chance to make a good first impression. Therefore, follow the appropriate conventions of writing a formal letter. Never simply scribble a handwritten note.

Figure 10.2 demonstrates the concise and focused nature and form of the cover letter.

OTHER TYPES OF APPLICATION

Application Forms

Many institutions have their own internal procedures for hiring staff, which can involve the use of a specific application form. This form allows the organization to obtain particular information regarding credentials and experience in a convenient and consistent format. Large and diverse organizations may also have targeted applications for various positions. A school board, for example, will have different forms for full- and part-time positions, substitute teaching, sports areas, secretarial support services, etc. In these cases, make sure that you submit the correct form.

Application forms come in many shapes and sizes, but online applications are a growing trend in North America. The applicant is sometimes offered a choice but can also be directed to use a single method: print an application form and fax/mail it in or complete the application form online and submit it

SHELLEY MARGARET BOSPEROUS

1245 Main Street, #25 • Anytown, NL A6D 3Y7
Home: 709-123-9876 • Cell: 709-321-6789 • smb2@localmail.ca

March 15, 2012

Mrs. Mary E. Allan
Assistant Recruiting Officer
Bythebook School Board
3670 Normal Road
Busytown, NL A5E 2X6

Dear Mrs. Allan:

It was a pleasure to talk with you last week at the Open Career Day hosted at the Riverpart Inn. Further to your suggestion, I am submitting my resumé for your consideration. As you may remember, I am currently completing my Bachelor of Education at Instructional University and am seeking a full-time classroom position for the upcoming fall term.

Bythebook School Board's aim to maximize every student's full academic potential regardless of background, culture, or social status deeply resonates with me. Therefore, I feel that I would make a solid contribution to any of your schools. However, in searching your website, I noticed that Rockville Elementary School offers a special program in the creative arts. I feel that my skills, which include an extensive background in amateur theatre and the ability to read music and play the piano, would especially benefit Rockville's students.

Again, thank you for your time last week. Please do not hesitate to contact me if you have any questions or wish to schedule an interview.

Yours truly,

Shelley M. Bosperous

Shelley M. Bosperous
Enclosure

Figure 10.2   Sample Cover Letter

electronically. The issue of electronic submissions is still under legal review in various jurisdictions due to the lack of a signature and concern with privacy laws. In any case, you must follow the procedures as demanded by the organization to which you are applying.

Here are a few considerations regarding application forms:

- Read all instructions carefully before you fill in any spaces. If the form says to use black ink, use black ink. If you must include a handwritten piece, don't attach a typed version. Instructions matter and you are ill-advised to dismiss them.
- Print your answers rather than using cursive script. Make sure that your printing is clear. The last thing you want is to have someone struggling to decipher your writing.
- Answer every question fully or to the best of your ability. If you are asked to provide something you do not have, print "pending," "not yet acquired," "not available," or "N/A." Don't leave the line blank.
- In some cases, you will be asked to check or block in boxes to indicate your answers. Make sure that all such marks are clean, neat, and in the appropriate locations.
- Many application forms require contact numbers, your signature, and the date completed. Do not forget to provide this information; otherwise, your application will not be processed.
- Unless asked to attach a specific document, do not attach anything. Don't take it upon yourself to include your CV, resumé, or references.
- You may be asked to submit your application to a processing agency at a different address than the organization or to send it by registered mail or courier. Make sure that you follow the delivering instructions carefully.

Electronic Applications

Many educational employers now list opportunities on online job boards or their own websites, where they might also include application criteria and procedures. In many cases, employers also welcome e-mail applications. These suggested guidelines will help you when e-mailing applications:

- **Type your cover letter as an e-mail message.** Because you want your cover letter to get immediate attention, don't send it as an attachment. Wherever possible, address the message to a specific person.

- **Clearly state your purpose.** Indicate whether you are responding to a particular position the organization has advertised or applying for any available opportunity. If you are applying for a specific position, the e-mail's subject line should immediately tell the reader what you are applying for, such as "Application for Substitute Teacher, file number 360."

- **Include your resumé as an attachment.** That way, you can be sure that the format appears exactly as you have designed it.

- **Print your message and look at it carefully before sending it.** Typographical errors or missing words are often harder to catch on the screen than on the printed page. Another editing strategy is to send the e-mail to yourself first so that you can see how your message looks and ensure that the attachment opens as it should. This practice also allows you to see your e-mail as your reader will.

- **Keep a copy of your final submissions.** In this way, you have a record of what was sent and on what date. A copy will be stored in your Sent folder, but you might prefer to blind carbon copy yourself on the e-mail.

- **Always use an appropriate e-mail account.** You may have multiple accounts, and some of them may have usernames like "imtheman" or "snugglebunny" that amuse your friends. However, an informal username won't impress potential employers.

PERSONAL SECURITY AND CONFIDENTIALITY

Technology makes creating and submitting job applications much easier than in the past. Your CV, resumés, and cover letters can be easily stored and updated electronically. Submitting an application through an online form or e-mail makes the process much faster. However, you must be extremely careful with the information you include in printed and electronic documents.

The federal and provincial governments have enacted strict laws regarding what information is germane. Listed below are a few confidentiality concerns:

- **Age and date of birth:** Various provincial and federal regulations forbid discrimination on the basis of age; therefore, except in unusual circumstances, age should not be a factor in employment.

- **Citizenship/Place of birth:** This information is required only if Canadian citizenship or other form of official status is a condition of employment.

- **Credit score:** There is no need for any employer to delve into your credit history unless the position deals with financial obligations.
- **Gender:** Gender is not to be considered in employment, except in rare circumstances (e.g., affirmative action).
- **Legal issues:** You are under no obligation to inform prospective employers that you are in the middle of divorce proceedings or involved in a small claims court case.
- **Marital status/Living arrangements:** In certain special cases, private religious schools may (and are allowed to) ask for this information; otherwise, your personal life is outside the purview of your employer.
- **Medical conditions:** This issue can be problematic. For example, if a prospective teacher uses a wheelchair, the school will need to be properly equipped. Educational institutions may also require a medical examination by their own medical practitioners as a condition of employment.
- **Religious beliefs:** Unless seeking employment in an identified religious environment, you don't need to state your spiritual beliefs.
- **Social insurance number:** This number is given to an employer after you've been hired and is used for payroll purposes only.

Many hiring agencies and public organizations also check an applicant's activity on social media sites such as Facebook. This practice is a legal grey area, but there are currently no federal or provincial laws preventing access to what you've posted on such sites. Therefore, be forewarned that what you put on the Internet is open to scrutiny from all possible employers.

SOME FINAL WORDS ON CVs, RESUMÉS, AND APPLICATIONS

Applying for a teaching job or a related position can be somewhat nerve-racking. However, your first contact with a potential employer must be a positive one. In many cases, this introduction will be via your application, which will likely be one of many. It must pass an initial screening process before it is considered seriously. Therefore, it is essential that you take pride in these submissions and ensure that they look professional, are free of errors, and exhibit the highest standards.

CHAPTER 11

Giving an Oral Presentation

OBJECTIVES

- To prepare and deliver an oral presentation
- To use a script to your best advantage
- To enhance presentations with technology

INTRODUCTION

For some education students (and even seasoned teachers), the prospect of giving an oral presentation can be terrifying. The reason some people dread public speaking is almost always that they are afraid of appearing foolish by not knowing what to say or how to answer questions. But there is no reason you can't give a good presentation even if you're nervous—you just have to be prepared.

If you think about all the poor presentations you've attended, you can probably identify certain similarities: the speaker jumped from topic to topic, ignored crucial segments of an argument, assumed that the audience had certain knowledge about the subject, spoke in a muffled manner, or used slides and other technology that confused the group. The effective sessions you've attended were likely well organized, focused, and systematic.

Some individuals may be naturally more comfortable in front of an audience than others, and such individuals may indeed have a slight psychological advantage when it comes to oral presentations. However, as a future educator, you will find that many forms of public speaking will become a feature of your job. Not only will you speak to you class on a daily basis, but you also might address large groups of parents or colleagues regarding various educational matters. By following a few simple instructions, you can achieve positive results with any group.

PREPARING YOUR PRESENTATION

The general rule regarding oral presentations is that the more you know and the better prepared you are, the easier the task will be. Therefore, the worst thing that you can do is "wing it"; such lack of preparation almost always has disastrous results. Whether you are preparing a class lecture or a presentation to peers concerning an educational issue, leading a workshop for colleagues, or summarizing a conference event, the chances of success dramatically increase with careful and thoughtful preparation.

Ask Yourself Three Questions

As soon as you know that you have to give an oral presentation, ask yourself these three key questions:

- Who is my audience?
- What are my time frames (to prepare and to present)?
- What is my purpose?

Your responses to these questions will frame the length and breadth of your planning, determine the background research, focus the information, and guide you in deciding the actual practicalities of the presentation. After all, if you have to give a 15-minute conference summary tomorrow, your preparation will be vastly different than if you have to address 75 parents about report card changes in four weeks' time. Once you have the answers to these three questions, you can officially begin the planning process.

Consider the Basic Elements

All oral presentations, be they formal or informal, consist of three basic elements: an introduction, body (or content), and a conclusion. Each element will expand and take on different orientations depending on the audience, topic, and time limits. However, each must be prepared.

Introduction. The main purpose of any introduction is to set the scene and give the audience the following information:

- your name
- your status/qualifications
- the general orientation of your presentation
- any necessary background information

- the main goal(s) of the presentation
- an overview of the topic(s) to be addressed
- the method(s) that you will use

Body/content. Of course, this element is the most important part of your presentation and can take any number of forms:

- explaining
- supporting
- presenting
- defending
- contrasting
- debating
- raising issues

Conclusion. Never allow any presentation to simply fade away. Consider these points when concluding your presentations:

- A clear and focused summary highlights the issues raised in the introduction and body without including new information.
- Depending on the topic and orientation, an emotional summary may be appropriate, especially if further action is required.
- A summary of recommendations and possibilities is also a positive way to conclude a presentation.
- A summary must not create a dead end where no further thought is necessary.

Know Your Topic

For the purposes of your presentation, you are the expert and will probably know more about your topic than many members of the audience. You need to show that your grasp of the subject matter goes beyond what you include in your talk. If you present everything, you won't be able to answer questions. The more background reading you do, the more information you will have to fall back on when someone asks you a question.

Consider Your Audience

In some cases, it could be a mistake to prepare a presentation based on what you know about your topic. You might want to approach the talk from precisely the opposite direction, from the point of view of the audience. How much will the typical audience member know about this topic? What will he or she find most interesting? Most relevant? What can you take for granted as common knowledge in the context? If you combine these questions with one of your own—What do I want my audience to know?—you have the basis for setting up your talk.

Plan to Speak Rather Than Read

Giving a presentation involves much more than writing an essay and then reading it to a group of people. In fact, many of the least successful presentations are those where presenters simply assume that they can read a prepared paper. This approach fails to engage the audience and generally leads to inattention and disinterest.

To keep your presentations interesting, try these strategies:

- **Don't write out everything you plan to say.** Unless you are a skilled reader, the presentation will sound laboured and monotonous. Instead, write down only the main talking points to guide you through your talk and keep you on track.
- **Prepare notes—perhaps on index cards—for each issue that you plan to discuss.** Because you can't read rough notes to your audience, you will be forced to use your own words and, likely, a more natural speaking style. Make sure, however, that you write clearly and large enough to be able to read your notes.
- **Start off well.** If you are worried that you may freeze at the beginning of your talk or you want to give your introductory statement in a forceful manner, write out the first paragraph of what you want to say, just to get you started.
- **Consider preparing an outline for your audience.** This handout will give your audience something to follow along with as you talk. Typically, you would base this outline on the one you use to organize your presentation, but you may want to include additional details and a bibliography for your audience.
- **Use appropriate visual aids.** Visual aids can attract and focus the audience's attention. If you are likely to become self-conscious when standing in front of a group, you will be more at ease when all eyes are on your visual aids and not on you. Visuals also provide another form of lecture notes to remind you of what you want to say. Creating a PowerPoint or Pages presentation gives you the flexibility to present your information in a variety of ways for maximum effect.

- **Rehearse your talk.** The more you practise your talk, the smoother your presentation will be when you deliver it to your audience. Trial runs will show you where the weak points are and let you know if you're running over or under time.

USING VISUAL AIDS

With the availability of graphic presentation software, laptop computers, and video projectors, your ability to use visual aids in a presentation is limited only by your imagination. For instance, you could develop a PowerPoint or Pages presentation that includes video clips and sound as well as animated diagrams. Even if you don't have access to these or similar programs, you can create overhead transparencies that highlight the main points of your talk and include pictures and diagrams. The following suggestions apply to any visuals that you might want to display.

Keep It Simple
Simplicity is the cardinal rule and applies to every aspect of your visual aids. It is much better to put too little material on a slide than too much. Do not overload the audience with technology.

- **Use plain fonts.** Unless you need a fancy one for a specific reason, stick with fonts that are easy to read. Avoid fonts that are too elaborate—they have reduced readability and can become irritating.
- **Choose an appropriate font size.** The last thing you want on your slides or overheads is text that is too small to decipher. The regular 12-point font you use for your papers will be too small when it is projected on a screen. The minimum size you can use will depend to some extent on the size of the room, but one rule of thumb suggests 36 point for titles and 24 for body text. It's always a good idea to test your presentation in the room where you'll be presenting your talk so that you can make adjustments if necessary.
- **Use a simple background.** If you're using PowerPoint or Pages to make your slides, choose a plain background and use the same one on every slide.
- **Don't overuse colour or animation.** Unless you have a good reason for doing so, avoid multicoloured slides or animation effects that are too busy or distracting.

- **Keep sounds to a minimum.** Remember that background music and other sounds can be a distraction.
- **Don't put too much information on one slide.** If you treat your slides as a script, you'll be tempted to read directly from them. Instead, make your point briefly on the slide and then expand on the material as you talk. This will make your presentation sound much more natural and professional. If you have a diagram or graph, use the simplest version that you can.
- **Don't use too many slides.** A common weakness in presentations is the overuse of slides, suggesting that the speaker cannot manage to talk without a prop. At the beginning of your presentation, try to establish a rapport with the audience by talking briefly without a slide. Then, after you finish your last slide, try to put the focus back on you as a person talking to other people, even if you speak as a representative of an organization. Some situations may even prevent the use of any technological aids. For example, if you are one of three presenters commenting on a recent conference, the use of vast amounts of media may be inappropriate.

Keep It Organized

The second fundamental rule of using visual aids is to make sure that your material is well organized. If you use a consistent organizational scheme, the audience will become used to it and will be able to follow along more easily.

- **Begin with a title slide.** A title slide sets the tone and orients the audience to your topic. It should contain the title, your name, and other main data.
- **Create a summary slide.** This will give an outline of your talk so that your audience knows what to expect.
- **Use headings and subheadings.** Most of your slides should be in point form, using numbers or bullets, with headings and subheadings. With this layout, the audience will be able to distinguish your main points from elaborations.
- **Consider section breaks.** If your talk falls naturally into several sections, you could start each one with a new title slide. Anything that allows the audience to see the structure of your talk is worth doing.
- **Keep your overheads in order.** If you are using overhead transparencies, make sure that they are in the correct order and orientation when you start and keep them in an ordered pile as you

use them. You may have to refer to one later, and you don't want to be shuffling through a disorganized heap to find the one you want.

Keep Copyright in Mind

 The use of other peoples' visual materials, such as figures, tables, and segments from TV programs, newscasts, and documentaries, is a complicated legal and moral issue. As with your essays and other forms of writing, representing other people's work or ideas as your own is plagiarism and can have serious consequences. Although most material can be used with proper acknowledgement, some might not be so open to third-party use.

The rules regarding copyright are changing regularly and impact different media in varying ways. The matter is further complicated by the specific regulations that exist within each organization, including universities, colleges, and school boards. It is your responsibility to learn and follow these guidelines.

MAKING YOUR PRESENTATION

Dress Comfortably

Dressing comfortably means not overdressing but also not dressing down for the occasion. For a presentation that simulates a more formal occasion, you will be expected to dress accordingly. On the other hand, your usual clothing may be completely appropriate for most student presentations.

Give Yourself Time at the Beginning

If you have equipment to set up or other preparations to make, be sure to do so before the session begins. Always have a back-up plan in the event of a technological disaster. We've all attended presentations where something went wrong—the computer program was incompatible, the presenter brought the wrong cable, or the room wasn't dark enough to see the visual aids. If you can identify and either fix or adapt to such problems beforehand, you won't get flustered trying to resolve them in front of your audience.

Begin with an Overview

If the audience knows how the talk is structured, they will be able to understand what you are doing as you move from one point to another. Introduce your topic and then give a brief statement of the main areas you will discuss. Again, an overhead or handout is useful because the audience can refer to it as your talk progresses.

If you do use a handout as a guide, remember that distribution is important. When will you give out the papers? How will you use them? Additionally, this document must be free of any grammatical and spelling errors, be clear, and be targeted specifically to your presentation. If you would like to leave your audience with some questions or issues to contemplate, these can be easily added to your handout.

Project Your Voice

The delivery of your presentation is just as important as the contents. When you speak, remember these rules:

- Don't mumble—make sure that everyone can hear you.
- Don't speak too quickly.
- Don't mispronounce words.
- Don't speak in a monotone—put some feeling into what you say.
- Don't remain static—move around a bit, if possible.

Commence Powerfully

The worst way to start a talk is by saying something like "You'll have to forgive me, I'm really nervous about this" or "I hope this projector is going to work properly." Even if you are nervous, create an air of confidence.

Maintain Eye Contact with Your Audience

Look around the room as you speak. Don't stare at your notes or some point at the back of the room. When you look at individuals, you involve them in what you are saying. As you scan the faces in front of you, you can also monitor for signs of boredom or incomprehension and adjust your talk accordingly.

Work with Your Visual Aids

If you have visual aids, take advantage of them; just remember that the visual material should only enhance your talk, not deliver it for you. Some of the following guidelines may help you when you are using visual aids:

- When you are making a point from your overhead or slide, try to use different words and expand on what is there. Don't just parrot the information.
- Give your audience enough time to read through each visual. They will find it frustrating to see images, overheads, or slides flash by before they've had a chance to take them in.

- Explain your figures. If it's a graph, describe what the x- and y-axes represent, and then explain what the graph shows. If it's another type of illustration, take the audience through it step by step. You may be familiar with the material, but your audience might not be.

Don't Go Too Fast

A good talk is one that is well paced. If you're discussing background information that everyone is familiar with, you can go over it a little faster; if you're describing something complex or less familiar, go slowly. It often helps to explain a complicated point a couple of times in slightly different ways. A personal or professional narrative can also provide context. Don't be afraid to ask your audience if they understand. Almost certainly, someone will speak up if there is a problem.

Monitor Your Time Allotment

As well as pacing your delivery, you must ensure that you aren't going to finish too quickly or, worse, go over your allotted time. If you've rehearsed your talk and timed it properly, you should know roughly how long it will take. Remember to allow extra time for questions that people might ask during your talk. Ideally, you should plan to make your talk a little shorter than the amount of time you have available so that you have some leeway to answer questions.

End Strongly

As mentioned earlier, don't let your talk simply trail off at the end. Summarize your main points and draw some conclusions. These inferences should be available on your visual material and/or noted on your handout. Raising some questions in your conclusions will also set up the question period to follow.

Be Prepared for Questions

The question period is a time when you can really make a good impression. Fielding questions gives you an opportunity to demonstrate your thorough understanding of the topic and even to reinforce one or two points that you think you may have missed. If you know your material well, you should have no problem dealing with the content of the questions, but the manner in which you answer these questions is important, too:

- When a question is asked, try to move a bit towards the questioner and pay close attention to what he or she is asking. Make eye contact and maintain a pose that shows interest in the question.

- It's a good idea to repeat a question if you are in a large room where everyone may not have heard it. Doing so might also solidify the question in your mind, reaffirm the questioner that you've understood him or her, and give you a few extra moments to consider possible responses.
- If you didn't hear or didn't understand a question, don't be afraid to ask the person to repeat or clarify it.
- Keep your answers short and to the point. Rambling answers are not helpful to anyone.
- If you don't know an answer, say so. It's okay to admit that you don't know everything—as long as you don't do so for every question. And it's definitely better to admit that you don't know an answer than to guess or make up a response that everyone will know is incorrect.

Be Human

As social beings, we naturally want to be entertained. An oral presentation should not be seen as a comedic or theatrical event, but there is no reason why the most serious of subjects cannot be treated with humanity and care. When appropriate, don't be afraid to tell a story, insert a poetic reference, quote a noted intellectual, or even ask your audience to consider some over-arching issues.

CHAPTER 12

Active Listening

OBJECTIVES

- To understand the value of active listening
- To use active listening for deeper comprehension
- To appreciate active listening as a professional tool, particularly with children and adolescents

INTRODUCTION

Before humans could communicate with symbols or writing, they relied on their speaking and listening skills. Even with advancements in the written word and technology, effective verbal communication—especially listening—remains a valuable asset for educators. The ability to be an active listener, to understand what someone says and to react appropriately, will make you a much better educator and, in many ways, a more engaged and responsible citizen.

THE ART OF LISTENING

Listening and speaking are highly complex and personal tasks. Unlike writing, verbal communication is a more immediate and emotional exchange. It also comprises a large part of our lives. On an average day, we spend approximately 40 per cent of our time listening, 35 per cent speaking, 15 per cent reading, and 10 per cent writing (Burley-Allen, 1995). The percentage of time spent on verbal communication is even higher for daycare and elementary school teachers (90 to 95 per cent) and is approximately 70 per cent for middle and secondary school teachers and college and university instructors.

Although we spend the majority of our day speaking and listening, we might not be very good at either. We've all been in situations (professional or social) where the person we were speaking to was obviously uninterested in what we were saying. Maybe he or she was texting, gazing into space, or even looking for an excuse to end the conversation. Or perhaps we are the culprits, only partially listening to our parents, daydreaming during class lectures, or ignoring someone because his or her stories are too long.

One factor that affects our ability to listen is a focus on speaking. Are you guilty of listening only to find an opportunity to express your own opinion? Do you ever raise your voice to indicate that what you heard (or thought you heard) was without merit or foundation? If so, the following strategies will help you be a more active listener.

ACTIVE LISTENING STRATEGIES

As active-listening theories have evolved, so too have the ways that educators view listening. It is generally accepted that teachers do not listen as intently as they should and that, with more developed listening skills, they will be better able to manage their own educational environment and engage their students (regardless of age level) in deeper ways. While highlighting different aspects, a number of listening strategies strive to make the practising educator a better listener.

One such strategy is the LINK method: listen actively, invite personal interest, notice and pay attention, and know the speaker as an individual. On the other hand, communication scholar Marisue Pickering (1986) suggests that there are four characteristics of empathetic listeners:

- a desire to be other-directed rather than forcing one's own feelings and ideas onto another
- a desire to be non-defensive and open to others rather than attempting to protect oneself
- a desire to imagine roles, perspectives, and/or experiences of the other rather than assuming that all experiences match the listener
- a desire to listen as a receiver and not as a critic, with a desire to understand the other individual rather than attempting to change that person (p. 17)

Pickering also identifies 10 specific skills associated with active listening (see Table 12.1).

Whatever active listening strategy you follow, keep in mind that you won't use every skill in every situation. Just as you write for a specific audience, you will also adjust your listening skills to the specific context. After all, a daycare teacher, a high-school mathematics teacher, and an economics professor listen

Table 12.1 Empathetic Listening Skills

Skill	Empathetic Action
Acknowledging	Providing verbal and/or non-verbal awareness of the other (e.g., maintaining eye contact).
Paraphrasing	Responding to a person's basic verbal message (e.g., "Do you mean . . .?").
Reflecting	Returning feelings, experiences, or content heard or seen through cues (e.g., posture, facial expression, body language).
Interpreting	Offering a tentative/measured interpretation about the person's feelings and/or situation (e.g., "Well, in my view . . .").
Summarizing	Bringing together the overall conversation; suggesting an overview without judging.
Probing	Eliciting greater detail and/or clarification by asking questions in a supportive way.
Providing feedback	Sharing perceptions, reactions, and relevant experiences and expertise; becoming closer to the speaker.
Supporting	Showing care and a sense of bonding with the speaker (e.g., "I know how you feel about . . .").
Verifying perceptions	Using neutral questions to clarify the speaker's situation and position.
Being quiet	Giving the speaker enough time to talk and consider the situation.

Source: Adapted from Pickering, M. (1986). Communication. *Explorations, 3*(1), pp. 16–19.

to their respective students in particular ways. The environment surrounding any speaking–listening dyad shifts quickly, but the active listener is able to adapt accordingly. However, regardless of the situation, he or she is always listening in an appropriate manner.

ACTIVE LISTENING WITH CHILDREN AND ADOLESCENTS

As an educator, you will encounter unique situations when listening to children and adolescents. In some cases, a student may not have the vocabulary required to explain the situation. Other students may become so emotional that coherent speech is impossible. Remember the following points when speaking and listening to your students:

- Children and adolescents can quickly detect disinterest, and you will find yourself excluded from their circle if you do not show real interest in what they say. You don't have to agree with them, but you must listen fully and intently.
- Listen with an open mind and be alert to nuances in the conversation. Never half-listen to children or adolescents. It is even more important that you be open and aware when communicating with students whose command of the English language may be weak and/or those who come from a culture with different values.
- Your students will often assume that you know the specific context of their topic and all the people involved. If you don't, politely interrupt to ask questions. You will clarify the matter and help (re) focus the speaker.
- Give the speaker your full attention. Teachers have a habit of half-listening as they keep tabs on the rest of the class or are on their way to a meeting. Although you will have many responsibilities, it is essential that you focus on the student so that he or she feels valued.
- Don't judge. As with any active listening, it is not your place to judge the speaker's actions or situation. Bear in mind that you are receiving only one point of view; therefore, your professional actions must not be guided by this single event. Be empathetic, not judgmental.
- Listen for any indication that the student is involved in bullying, a growing dilemma in education. Many schools and educational facilities are developing policies to deal with this issue. One method is to employ active listening.

SUMMARY

You may already have some active listening skills in your repertoire. Others, however, might be harder to master. For example, you might find it difficult to resist the temptation to advise, disagree, or interrupt. Working on these skills and being an active listener shows that you respect and value the speaker. When you truly listen to others, they may begin to trust you more. Active listening not only allows you to express generosity towards people, but it also strengthens your attention span, cognitive abilities, and capacity for compassion.

REFERENCES

Burley-Allen, M. (1995). *Listening: The forgotten skill*. New York, NY: Wiley.
Pickering, M. (1986). Communication. *Explorations*, 3(1), pp. 16–19.

CHAPTER 13

Writing a Formal Letter and E-mail

OBJECTIVES

- To recognize the importance of a well-written formal letter
- To understand the proper structure of formal letters
- To appreciate the need for handwriting in education
- To follow guidelines when using e-mail

INTRODUCTION

Formal letters and e-mail messages are important types of writing for any educator. As such, they must be treated as professional documents with specific rules. Knowing these conventions is an essential skill that will help you throughout your career.

THE FORMAL LETTER

Although quicker and easier forms of communication have evolved, the old-fashioned formal letter is going to be around for some time. For all its inherent slowness, the letter is still an effective way to communicate because it is written with a clear intent: to describe something, demand action, present a case, and/or make a plea. A letter is also considered more meaningful than an e-mail because it generally takes longer to write and demands greater energy and thought.

Writing formal letters remains a significant element of a teacher's professional life. Along with the report letter/memo and cover letter that we discussed in previous chapters, educators may also write reference letters and letters to their local union, government representative, or school board about various education issues. Because you will write many such letters, it is important that you understand how a formal letter is organized.

A formal letter is generally no longer than two pages. The text should be set flush left and include the following components:

- sender's address
- date
- recipient's name, job title, and address
- salutation
- body
- closing
- sender's signature, name, and job title

Sender's Address

The first item of a formal letter is the sender's address. If appropriate, you can include this information by using your employer's letterhead. Remember, though, that doing so means that you are representing the organization. Letters on official letterhead carry a degree of seriousness and trust that is not intended for more personal correspondence. Alternatively, you can use certain computer software to design your own stationery.

Date

Every formal letter includes the date on which it was written. The various styles for writing dates can cause confusion. For example, does 6/4/11 mean June 4, 2011, or April 6, 2011? Dates are important in educational circles because they help to chart events and note progress. One way to avoid confusion is to write out the date, such as June 4, 2011, or 4 June 2011. (Note that the first format includes a comma between the date and the year, but the second does not.) Whichever style you use, don't abbreviate the month or the year.

Recipient's Name, Title, and Address

In formal communication, include the recipient's full name and title (Ms., Mrs., Mr., Dr., Rev., etc.). *Miss* is generally no longer used to refer to an unmarried woman; however, follow the recipient's preference whenever possible. Also include the person's job title (e.g., Vice-President, Sales; Principal, Brookside Secondary School)—this information may not be necessary if, for example, you are writing to a parent.

Letters can, of course, be written to more than one person, as long as the recipients reside at the same address. When writing to parents who live together, it is acceptable to address a single letter to both. Separate letters would be necessary only if the parents have different residential addresses and share custody.

Be sure to provide the recipient's complete address, including postal or zip code, department unit or office number, and apartment or suite number. Failure to include the correct and full address could result in your letter being delivered late or being returned.

The use of abbreviations in addresses is open to some debate. For example, is 123 Main Street West or 123 Main St. W. the better method? As long as they are clear, standard address abbreviations are fine.

Salutation

A salutation is the opening of a formal letter. While you would include, for example, "Mr. Peter Smith" as the recipient's name in the previous section, here would you write "Dear Mr. Smith" followed by a colon. Avoid informal greetings, such as *Hi* or *Hello*. In a similar manner, don't be overly familiar. "Dear Peter" would be inappropriate, unless you know the recipient well and the letter is more personal.

If you are writing to an organization and don't know the recipient's name or gender, you may use the generic "Dear Sir or Madam." Although not as personal as being addressed by name or the proper title, this salutation is still appropriate.

Body

The "perfect" formal letter has three paragraphs that fit on one page. Of course, not every subject can be explained in such a concise manner. Just remember that a formal letter is not an essay; it is a tightly crafted and focused piece that details a specific matter. Therefore, clarity and brevity are two main elements in the construction of all such letters.

Generally speaking, the first paragraph of a formal letter is one or two sentences that state your purpose. The second (and others, if necessary) expands on the first by offering more detail and all relevant information. The final paragraph, which can be as short as the opening one, indicates the action or resolution that you expect to follow.

Formal letters can be forceful, but they should never be threatening or jarring in any way. Do not make unsubstantiated claims or suggest wild actions. Be respectful and stay focused on the task at hand.

Closing

At one time, closings included "Yours faithfully," "Yours in peace," or even "I am indebted to you." Today, the most common way to close a formal letter is to use "Yours truly" or "Yours sincerely," followed by the sender's signature and typed name below. If your recipient does not know you and might not be able to tell your gender from your first name, you can place "(Mr.)" or "(Ms.)" before your typed name. If appropriate, you can also include your credentials (Special Education Teacher, Unit Head, B.A., etc.) after your name.

Acceptable Abbreviations

Although the shorthand used on the Internet and in text messaging (OMG, LOL, U, etc.) is not to be used in formal letters, other abbreviations are permitted:

ASAP	as soon as possible
cc	carbon copy; placed at the end of a letter to indicate that copies have been sent to others, whose names are listed after the abbreviation; refers to when copies were made by using carbon paper
enc.	enclosed/enclosure; placed after the closing to indicate that additional documents have been attached to the original letter and, possibly, any carbon copies
pp	*per procurationem*; placed in the closing to indicate that the letter was not signed by the individual but by someone authorized to sign on his or her behalf
pto	please turn over; placed in the lower right corner of the page to indicate that a letter is printed double-sided
RSVP	please respond/reply requested

Further Guidelines

As with any type of professional or academic writing, the presentation of the piece is also important. Follow these rules when writing formal letters:

* Avoid using abbreviations and contractions, except for special considerations (see the previous section).
* Avoid using slang, technical terminology, and unfamiliar words unless they are germane to the issue.
* Use action verbs; avoid the passive verb *to be*.
* Use *I* where appropriate.

- Make sure that your letter is free of grammar, spelling, and punctuation errors.
- Avoid underlining, bolding, and italics. Use a standard font style and size, such as Times New Roman 12.
- Single space the letter and leave spaces between paragraphs and the various components.
- For letters that are longer than one page, number the subsequent pages and staple all the pages together. You can also print the letter double-sided. Use a paper clip for any enclosures.
- Avoid coloured paper. A formal letter is not an artistic statement but a serious written communication. White bond paper is the best type to use, especially if the recipient wishes to make photocopies. If you're using an organization's letterhead, use it for only the first page; use paper of a similar quality and colour for any subsequent pages.

HANDWRITING

During the early twentieth century, handwriting was a staple of the North American school curriculum. Students were usually taught printing in the early grades and initial cursive writing in middle school. Individual writing styles developed during secondary school. Until recently, all school work was handwritten, with penmanship graded and displayed on a regular basis. There were many handwriting programs developed during this time, each with their own manuals, practice books, teaching aids, and evaluation standards. The three main programs still used in North America are the Zaner-Bloser (the oldest and most widely used), the D'Nealian script (an adaptation of the original 1894 Palmer method), and the relatively new Getty–Dubay script.

At one time, teacher candidates across North America took classes in blackboard writing. They were trained to print and write on a board so that everyone in the class could read the words. They were also taught to move the chalk across the board without making it squeak and, conversely, how to quiet a noisy classroom by making the chalk squeak.

Teachers continue to use handwriting on a daily basis, writing notes on student projects, jottings in agendas or meeting handouts, comments on SMART Boards, replies to memos from colleagues, and responses to parent requests, as well as filling out any number of forms that are not available electronically. During the last decade, however, the importance of teaching good penmanship has declined in favour of teaching keyboarding skills.

For example, the Indiana Department of Education removed the teaching of cursive writing from its list of mandatory courses in 2011. However, due to a somewhat unanticipated backlash, the state's legislature is considering reversing the decision (State of Indiana, 2012).

The North American debate over the roles of cursive writing and keyboarding is an emerging issue. How can teachers deal with both forms? As new teachers, you will be actively involved in this discussion and may well help shape the outcome.

E-MAIL

There is no question that e-mail, along with other forms of electronic communication, is here to stay. However, its place within the formal educational landscape is still being formulated. Issues such as personal privacy, professional responsibility, and parental involvement require clarification. Over time, these and other issues will be resolved as schools, organizations, and the courts set procedures. Meanwhile, educators can use the following points as guidelines when writing e-mail messages:

- Keep your professional and personal e-mails completely separate. Set up different e-mail accounts and use each one for only its intended purpose. Most education institutions provide staff members with an e-mail account that is maintained by the organization. It is understood that this account will be used solely for work-related activities. Simply put, don't use your work e-mail (or, for that matter, your work's Internet) to chat with friends or arrange your vacation. As mentioned in Chapter 10, avoid "sexy" or "crude" usernames for your e-mail accounts.

- Until the laws are clarified, it is unwise to engage in private communication with a current or former student via e-mail or social media site, especially when the student is a minor. Unlike a report card, this form of communication bypasses parents. As the teacher and adult in this situation, it is essential that you keep appropriate authoritative distance.

- If you receive an e-mail that requires you to take action (such as contacting youth protection agencies, the school principal, or police), you must do so. Bear in mind that an e-mail carries legal weight and cannot be dismissed simply because its medium is electronic.

- Never say anything in an e-mail that you would not say to the recipient in person.
- Respond to every work-related message. The general rule of thumb is to reply within 24 hours of receiving an e-mail. When replying, use the "Reply All," "Cc," and "Bcc" functions only when necessary.
- Every e-mail, and certainly every professional message, must be devoid of grammar and spelling errors. Don't use all capital letters or symbols that might indicate anger or other emotions.
- Avoid all icons and other adornments in professional e-mails. Your reader might find them distracting.
- Include attachments only when germane to the issue at hand. E-mails can easily become loaded with irrelevant attachments, which readers can find tiresome.

REFERENCES

State of Indiana. (2012). Senate Bill 83. Retrieved from http://www.in.gov/legislative/bills/2012/IN/IN0083.1.html

CHAPTER 14

Common Errors in Grammar and Usage

OBJECTIVES

- To identify the parts of speech
- To understand the various sentence structures
- To avoid common problems in grammar and usage

INTRODUCTION

This chapter is not a comprehensive grammar lesson but a survey of those areas where students most often make mistakes. It will help you pinpoint weaknesses as you edit your work. Once you fall into the habit of checking your work, it won't be long before you are correcting potential problems as you write.

The terms used here are the most basic and familiar ones. For more information, check the glossary. If you're interested in a more exhaustive treatment, consult one of the many books that deal exclusively with grammar and usage.

PARTS OF SPEECH

Traditional English grammar is made up of eight parts of speech:

adjective: A word that modifies a noun or pronoun and is usually placed before the word it modifies (e.g., *small, intelligent, warm*).
adverb: A word that modifies a verb, adjective, phrase, clause, or another adverb. An adverb can answer the question *how? when? where?* or *why?* and often ends in *-ly* (e.g., *partly, soon, rarely*).

conjunction: A word that joins phrases and/or clauses together. The most common conjunctions are *and, or, but, for,* and *so.*

interjection: A word or short phrase that indicates emotion, usually accompanied by an exclamation mark (e.g., *Oh no! Wow!*). Interjections are rarely used in formal or academic writing.

noun: A word that represents a person, place, proper name, or thing (e.g., *teacher, home, Dmitri*).

preposition: A word that links nouns, pronouns, and phrases with other words to form a complete sentence (e.g., *of, about, to*).

pronoun: A word that replaces a noun (e.g., *he, it, we*).

verb: A word that expresses action (e.g., *run, sing, jump*).

Using all the parts of speech correctly will enhance your writing and help you understand sentence structure.

SENTENCE STRUCTURES

Along with the parts of speech, the basic tool in writing is the sentence. There are three kinds of sentences: simple, compound, and complex.

A simple sentence consists of a subject, a verb, and a modifier.

He ran quickly.

A compound sentence consists of all the parts of a simple sentence, along with two or more independent clauses joined by a conjunction.

He ran quickly to the library, but it was closed when he arrived.

A complex sentence contains one independent clause and at least one dependent clause.

Although I ran to the library with Peter, I did not want to go.

GRAMMAR AND USAGE ERRORS

Sentence Unity

SENTENCE FRAGMENTS

To be complete, a sentence must have both a subject and a verb in an independent clause; if it doesn't, it's a fragment. There are times in informal writing when it is acceptable to use a sentence fragment in order to give emphasis to a point:

✓ Will the government try to abolish the Senate? <u>Not likely</u>.

Here the sentence fragment *Not likely* is clearly intended to be understood as a short form of *It is not likely that the government will try*. Unintentional sentence fragments, on the other hand, usually seem incomplete rather than shortened:

✗ I enjoy living in Vancouver. <u>Being a skier who likes the sea.</u>

The last "sentence" is incomplete because it lacks an independent clause with a subject and a verb. (Remember that a participle such as *being* is a *verbal*, or "part-verb," not a verb.) The fragment can be made into a complete sentence by adding a subject and a verb:

✓ <u>I am</u> a skier who likes the sea.

Alternatively, you could join the fragment to the preceding sentence:

✓ Being a skier who likes the sea, I enjoy living in Vancouver.

✓ I enjoy living in Vancouver, since I am a skier who likes the sea.

RUN-ON SENTENCES

A run-on sentence is one that continues beyond the point where it should have stopped:

✗ Mosquitoes and black flies are annoying, but they don't stop tourists from coming to spend their holidays in Canada, and such is the case in Ontario's northland.

This run-on sentence could be fixed by removing the word *and* and adding a period or semicolon after *Canada*.

Another kind of run-on sentence is one in which two independent clauses are wrongly joined by a comma. An independent clause is a phrase that can stand by itself as a complete sentence. Two independent clauses should not be joined by a comma without a coordinating conjunction:

✗ Northrop Frye won international acclaim as a critic, he was an English professor at the University of Toronto.

This error is known as a *comma splice*. There are three ways to correct it:

1. by putting a period after *critic* and starting a new sentence:

   ✓ . . . as a critic. He . . .

2. by replacing the comma with a semicolon:

   ✓ . . . as a critic; he . . .

3. by making one of the independent clauses subordinate to the other so that it doesn't stand by itself:

   ✓ Northrop Frye, who won international acclaim as a critic, was an English professor at the University of Toronto.

The one exception to the rule that independent clauses cannot be joined by a comma arises when the clauses are very short and arranged in a tight sequence:

   ✓ I opened the door, I saw the skunk, and I closed the door.

You should not use this kind of sentence very often.

Contrary to what many people think, words such as *however*, *therefore*, and *thus* cannot be used to join independent clauses:

   ✗ Two of my friends started out in the secondary program, however they quickly decided they didn't like working with adolescents.

This mistake can be corrected by beginning a new sentence after *secondary program* or (preferably) by replacing the comma with a semicolon:

   ✓ Two of my friends started out in the secondary program; however, they quickly decided they didn't like working with adolescents.

Another option is to join the two independent clauses with a coordinating conjunction—*and*, *or*, *nor*, *but*, *for*, *yet*, *so*, or *whereas*:

   ✓ Two of my friends started out in the secondary program, but they quickly decided they didn't like working with adolescents.

FAULTY PREDICATION

When the subject of a sentence is not grammatically connected to what follows (the predicate), the result is faulty predication:

   ✗   The <u>reason</u> he failed <u>was because</u> he couldn't handle multiple-choice exams.

The problem with this sentence is that *reason* and *was because* mean essentially the same thing. The subject is a noun and the verb *was* needs a noun clause to complete it:

   ✓   The <u>reason</u> he failed <u>was that</u> he couldn't handle multiple-choice exams.

Another solution is to rephrase the sentence:

   ✓   He failed because he couldn't handle multiple-choice exams.

Faulty predication also occurs with *is when* and *is where* constructions:

   ✗   The climax <u>is when</u> the servant discovers the body.

Again, you can correct this error in one of two ways:

1. Follow *is* with a noun phrase to complete the sentence:

   ✓   The climax <u>is the discovery</u> of the body by the servant.

   (or)

   ✓   The climax <u>is the servant's discovery</u> of the body.

2. Change the verb:

   ✓   The climax <u>occurs</u> when the servant discovers the body.

Subject–Verb Agreement

IDENTIFYING THE SUBJECT

A verb should always agree in number with its subject. Sometimes, however, when the subject does not come at the beginning of the sentence or when it is separated from the verb by other information, you may be tempted to use a verb form that does not agree:

✗ The <u>increase</u> in the rate for postage and materials <u>were condemned</u> by the teachers.

The subject here is *increase*, not *postage and materials*; therefore, the verb should be singular:

✓ The <u>increase</u> in the rate for postage and materials <u>was condemned</u> by the teachers.

Either, Neither, Each

The indefinite pronouns *either*, *neither*, and *each* always take singular verbs:

✓ <u>Neither</u> of the defendants <u>has</u> a trial date.

✓ <u>Each</u> of them <u>has</u> a lawyer.

Compound Subjects

When *or*, *either . . . or*, or *neither . . . nor* is used to create a compound subject, the verb should usually agree with the last item in the subject:

✓ Neither the professor nor <u>her students were</u> able to solve the equation.

✓ Either the students or <u>the TA was</u> misinformed.

You may find, however, that it sounds awkward in some cases to use a singular verb when a singular item follows a plural item:

orig. Either my history books or my biology <u>text is</u> going to gather dust this weekend.

In such instances, it's better to rephrase the sentence:

rev. This weekend, I'm going to ignore either my history books or my biology text.

Unlike the word *and*, which creates a compound subject and therefore takes a plural verb, the phrases *as well as* and *in addition to* do not create compound subjects; therefore, the verb remains singular:

✓ Tourtière <u>and</u> sugar pie <u>are</u> traditional Quebec dishes.

✓ Tourtière, <u>as well as</u> sugar pie, <u>is</u> a traditional Quebec dish.

COLLECTIVE NOUNS

A collective noun is a singular noun that comprises a number of members, such as *family*, army, or *team*. If the noun refers to the members as one unit, it takes a singular verb:

✓ The <u>team</u> <u>is</u> playing its first game tonight.

If, in the context of the sentence, the noun refers to the members as individuals, the verb becomes plural:

✓ The <u>team</u> <u>are</u> receiving their sweaters before the game.

✓ The <u>majority</u> of immigrants to Canada <u>settle</u> in cities.

TITLES

The title of a book or a movie or the name of a business or organization is always treated as a singular noun, even if it contains plural words; therefore, it takes a singular verb:

✓ John Dewey's <u>The Child and the Curriculum</u> <u>was</u> a bestseller.

✓ <u>Goodman & Goodman</u> <u>is</u> handling the school's accounting issues.

Verb Tenses

Native speakers of English usually know without thinking which verb tense to use in a given context. However, a few tenses can still be confusing.

THE PAST PERFECT

If the main verb is in the past tense and you want to refer to something that happened before that time, use the *past perfect* (*had* followed by the past participle). The time sequence will not be clear if you use the simple past in both clauses:

✗ He <u>hoped</u> that she <u>fixed</u> the printer.

✓ He <u>hoped</u> that she <u>had fixed</u> the printer.

Similarly, when you are reporting what someone said in the past—that is, when you are using *past indirect discourse*—you should use the past perfect tense in the clause describing what was said:

✗   He <u>told</u> the TA that he <u>wrote</u> the essay that week.

✓   He <u>told</u> the TA that he <u>had written</u> the essay that week.

USING *IF*

When you are describing a possibility in the future, use the present tense in the condition (*if*) clause and the future tense in the consequence clause:

✓   If he <u>tests</u> us on French verbs, I <u>will fail</u>.

When the possibility is unlikely, it is conventional—especially in formal writing—to use the *subjunctive* in the *if* clause, and *would* followed by the base verb in the consequence clause:

✓   If he <u>were</u> to cancel the test, I <u>would cheer</u>.

When you are describing a hypothetical instance in the past, use the *past subjunctive* (it has the same form as the past perfect) in the *if* clause and *would have* followed by the past participle for the consequence. A common error is to use *would have* in both clauses:

✗   If he <u>would have been</u> friendlier, I <u>would have asked</u> him to be my lab partner.

✓   If he <u>had been</u> friendlier, I <u>would have asked</u> him to be my lab partner.

WRITING ABOUT LITERATURE

When you are describing a literary work in its historical context, use the past tense:

✓   Margaret Atwood <u>wrote</u> *Surfacing* at a time when George Grant's *Technology and Empire* <u>was persuading</u> people to reassess technocratic values.

To discuss what goes on within a work of literature, however, you should use the present tense:

✓ The narrator <u>retreats</u> to the woods and <u>tries</u> to escape the rationalism of her father's world.

When you are discussing an episode or incident in a literary work and want to refer to a prior incident or a future one, use past or future tenses accordingly:

✓ The narrator <u>returns</u> to northern Quebec, where she <u>spent</u> her summers as a child; by the time she <u>leaves</u>, she <u>will have rediscovered</u> herself.

Be sure to return to the present tense when you have finished referring to events in the past or future.

Pronouns

PRONOUN REFERENCE

The link between a pronoun and the noun it refers to must be clear. If the noun doesn't appear in the same sentence as the pronoun, it should appear in the preceding sentence:

✗ The <u>textbook supply</u> in the bookstore had run out, so we borrowed <u>them</u> from the library.

Since *textbook* is used as an adjective rather than a noun, it cannot serve as referent or antecedent for the pronoun *them*. You must either replace *them* or change the phrase *textbook supply*:

✓ The <u>textbook supply</u> in the bookstore had run out, so we borrowed <u>the texts</u> from the library.

✓ The bookstore had run out of <u>textbooks</u>, so we borrowed <u>them</u> from the library.

When a sentence contains more than one noun, make sure there is no ambiguity about which noun the pronoun refers to:

✗ The public wants better <u>social services</u> along with lower <u>taxes</u>, but the government does not favour <u>them</u>.

What does the pronoun *them* refer to: the taxes, the social services, or both?

✓ The public wants better <u>social services</u> along with lower taxes, but the government does not advocate <u>spending increases</u>.

USING *IT* AND *THIS*
Using *it* and *this* without a clear referent can lead to confusion:

✗ Although the directors wanted to meet in January, <u>it</u> (<u>this</u>) didn't take place until May.

✓ Although the directors wanted to meet in January, <u>the conference</u> didn't take place until May.

Make sure that *it* or *this* clearly refers to a specific noun or pronoun.

USING *ONE*
People often use the word *one* to avoid overusing *I* in their writing. Although this practice is common in Britain, frequent use of *one* may seem too formal and even a bit pompous to Canadian and American audiences:

orig.   If <u>one</u> were to apply for the grant, <u>one</u> would find <u>oneself</u> engulfed in so many bureaucratic forms that <u>one's</u> patience would be stretched thin.

Even though there is nothing grammatically incorrect in this example, it may strike the reader as stiff or pretentious. The best thing to do is to recast the sentence with a plural subject:

rev.   If <u>researchers</u> were to apply for grants, <u>they</u> would find <u>themselves</u> engulfed in so many bureaucratic forms that <u>their</u> patience would be stretched thin.

Use *one* sparingly, and don't be afraid of the occasional *I*. Avoid mixing the third person *one* with the second person *you*:

✗ When <u>one</u> visits the Rocky Mountains, <u>you</u> are impressed by the grandeur of the scenery.

USING *ME* AND OTHER OBJECTIVE PRONOUNS

Remembering that it is wrong to say "Dorcas and me were invited to present our findings to the delegates" rather than "Dorcas and I were invited . . .," many people use the subjective form of the pronoun even when it should be objective:

✗ The delegates <u>invited</u> Dorcas and <u>I</u> to present our findings.

✓ The delegates <u>invited</u> Dorcas and <u>me</u> to present our findings.

The verb *invited* requires an object; *me* is the objective case. A good way to tell which form is correct is to ask yourself how the sentence would sound with only the pronoun. You will know by ear that the subjective form—"The delegates invited *I*"—is not appropriate.

The same problem often arises with prepositions, which should also be followed by a noun or pronoun in the objective case:

✗ <u>Between</u> you and <u>I</u>, this result doesn't make sense.

✓ <u>Between</u> you and <u>me</u>, this result doesn't make sense.

✗ Eating well is a problem <u>for we</u> students.

✓ Eating well is a problem <u>for us</u> students.

There are times, however, when the correct case can sound stiff or awkward:

orig. <u>To whom</u> was the award given?

Rather than using a correct but awkward form, try to reword the sentence:

rev. <u>Who received</u> the award?

The rule that a pronoun following a preposition takes the objective case has exceptions. When the preposition is followed by a clause, the pronoun should take the case required by its position in the clause:

✗ The students showed some concern <u>over whom</u> <u>would be selected</u> as dean.

Although the pronoun follows the preposition *over*, it is also the subject of the verb *would be selected* and therefore requires the subjective case:

> ✓ The students showed some concern <u>over</u> <u>who</u> <u>would be selected</u> as dean.

Similarly, when a *gerund* (a word that acts partly as a noun and partly as a verb) is the subject of a clause, the pronoun that modifies it takes the possessive case:

> ✗ We were surprised <u>by</u> <u>him</u> <u>dropping</u> out of school.

> ✓ We were surprised <u>by</u> <u>his</u> <u>dropping</u> out of school.

> ✗ He was tired <u>of</u> <u>me</u> <u>reminding</u> him.

> ✓ He was tired <u>of</u> <u>my</u> <u>reminding</u> him.

Modifiers

Adjectives modify nouns; adverbs modify verbs, adjectives, and other adverbs. Do not use an adjective to modify a verb:

> ✗ He played <u>good</u>. (adjective with verb)

> ✓ He played <u>well</u>. (adverb modifying verb)

> ✓ He played <u>really</u> <u>well</u>. (adverb modifying adverb)

> ✓ He had a <u>good</u> style. (adjective modifying noun)

> ✓ He had a <u>really</u> <u>good</u> style. (adverb modifying adjective)

SQUINTING MODIFIERS

Remember that clarity depends largely on word order: to avoid confusion, the connections between the different parts of a sentence must be clear. Modifiers should therefore be as close as possible to the words they modify. A squinting modifier is one that, because of its position, seems to look in two directions at once:

> ✗ She expected <u>after the announcement</u> a decline in the stock market.

Was *after the announcement* the time of expectation or the time of the market decline? Changing the order of the sentence or rephrasing it will make the meaning clearer:

✓ <u>After the announcement</u>, she expected a decline in the stock market.

✓ She expected the stock market to decline <u>after the announcement</u>.

Other squinting modifiers can be corrected in the same way:

✗ Our English professor gave a lecture on *Beowulf*, <u>which was well illustrated</u>.

✓ Our English professor gave a <u>well-illustrated lecture</u> on *Beowulf*.

Often the modifier works best when placed immediately in front of the phrase it modifies. Notice the difference that this placement can make:

<u>Only</u> she guessed the motive for the theft.

She <u>only</u> guessed the motive for the theft.

She guessed <u>only</u> the motive for the theft.

She guessed the motive for the theft <u>only</u>.

DANGLING MODIFIERS

Modifiers that have no grammatical connection with anything else in the sentence are said to be dangling:

✗ <u>Walking</u> around the campus in June, the river and trees made a picturesque scene.

Who is doing the walking? Here's another example:

✗ <u>Reflecting</u> on the results of the poll, it was decided not to announce the new tax cuts right away.

Who is doing the reflecting? Clarify the meaning by connecting the dangling modifier to a new subject:

✓   <u>Walking</u> around the campus in June, <u>Winnie</u> thought the river and trees made a picturesque scene.

✓   <u>Reflecting</u> on the results of the poll, <u>the government</u> decided not to announce the new tax cuts right away.

Pairs and Parallels

COMPARISONS

Make sure that your comparisons are complete. The second element in a comparison should be equivalent to the first, whether the equivalence is stated or merely implied:

✗   Today's students have a greater understanding of calculus than their parents.

This sentence suggests that the two things being compared are *calculus* and *parents*. Adding a second verb (*have*) equivalent to the first one shows that the two things being compared are parents' understanding and students' understanding:

✓   Today's students <u>have</u> a greater understanding of calculus than their parents <u>have</u>.

A similar problem arises in the following comparison:

✗   That new text is <u>a boring book</u> and so are the lectures.

The lectures may be boring, but they are not a boring book; to make sense, the two parts of the comparison must be parallel:

✓   The new text is <u>boring</u> and so are the lectures.

CORRELATIVES

Constructions such as *both . . . and*, *not only . . . but also*, and *neither . . . nor* are especially tricky. For the implied comparison to work, the two parts that come after the coordinating term must be grammatically equivalent:

✗ He <u>not only bakes</u> cakes <u>but also bread</u>.

✓ He bakes <u>not only cakes</u> <u>but also bread</u>.

PARALLEL PHRASING

A series of items in a sentence should be phrased in parallel wording. Make sure that all the parts of a parallel construction are in fact equal:

✗ We had to turn in <u>our rough notes</u>, <u>our calculations</u>, and <u>finished assignment</u>.

✓ We had to turn in <u>our rough notes</u>, <u>our calculations</u>, and <u>our finished assignment</u>.

Once you have decided to include the pronoun *our* in the first two elements, the third must have it too.

For clarity as well as stylistic grace, keep similar ideas in similar form:

✗ He <u>failed</u> economics and <u>barely passed</u> statistics, but political science <u>was</u> a subject he did well in.

✓ He <u>failed</u> economics and <u>barely passed</u> statistics but <u>did well</u> in political science.

Faulty parallelism is a common problem in bulleted or numbered lists:

✗ There are several reasons for purchasing this instructional model:
 - low <u>cost</u>
 - <u>there is</u> an instant rebate
 - <u>covered</u> by full one-year warranty
 - <u>getting</u> a free carrying case with your purchase

✓ There are several reasons for purchasing this model:
 - low <u>cost</u>
 - instant <u>rebate</u>
 - full one-year <u>warranty</u>
 - <u>carrying case</u>

CHAPTER 15

Punctuation and Style Treatments

OBJECTIVES

- To identify the 14 commonly used punctuation marks
- To illustrate how proper punctuation enhances written communication
- To introduce five kinds of type formats

INTRODUCTION

Punctuation is an area that causes people many problems. If your punctuation is faulty, your readers will be confused and may have to backtrack. Worse still, they may be tempted to skip over the rough spots. Punctuation marks are the critical traffic signals of writing; use them with precision to keep readers moving smoothly through your work.

Another part of writing that requires care is the use of type formats, particularly *boldface*, *highlighting*, *italics*, *font changes*, and *underlining*. These treatments, which can be easily implemented with most computer programs, must be used properly and judiciously.

PUNCTUATION

There are 14 commonly used punctuation marks, each with its own purposes and appropriate uses. In alphabetical order, these marks are *apostrophe*, *brackets*, *colon*, *comma*, *dash*, *ellipsis*, *exclamation mark*, *hyphen*, *parentheses*, *period*, *question mark*, *quotation marks*, *semicolon*, and *slash*.

Apostrophe [']

1. **Use an apostrophe to indicate possession.** The following rules are the easiest to remember:

   a) To illustrate the possessive, create an *of* phrase:

the girls fathers	→	the fathers <u>of the girls</u>
the childrens parents	→	the parents <u>of the children</u>
Shakespeares plays	→	the plays <u>of Shakespeare</u>

   b) If the noun in the *of* phrase ends in s, add an apostrophe:

   the girls' fathers

   c) If the noun in the *of* phrase does not end in s, add an apostrophe plus *s*:

   the children's parents

   Shakespeare's plays

2. **Use an apostrophe to show contractions of words:**

   isn't   we'll   he's   shouldn't   I'm

Don't confuse *it's* (the contraction of *it is*) with *its* (the possessive of *it*), which has no apostrophe. Remember that there is no such word as *its'*. Possessive pronouns never take an apostrophe: *yours, hers, its, ours, yours, theirs.*

Brackets [ ]

Brackets are square enclosures, not to be confused with parentheses (which are round). **Use brackets to set off a remark of your own within a quotation.** The brackets indicate that the words enclosed are not those of the person quoted:

Fox maintained, "Obstacles to Western unification [in the eighties] are as many as they are serious."

Brackets are sometimes used to enclose *sic*, which is used after an error, such as a misspelling, to show that the mistake was in the original. *Sic* may be italicized:

> The politician, in his letter to constituents, wrote about "these parlouse [*sic*] times of economic difficulty."

Use brackets sparingly. In other words, don't add explanations or extra information to quotations unless doing so will clarify the point for the reader.

Colon [:]

A colon indicates that something is to follow.

1. **Use a colon before a formal statement or series:**

   > ✓ The winners are the following: Anna, Dieter, George, and Hugh.

   Do not use a colon if the words preceding it do not form a complete sentence:

   > ✗ The winners are: Anna, Dieter, George, and Hugh.

   > ✓ The winners are Anna, Dieter, George, and Hugh.

   On the other hand, a colon often precedes a vertical list, even when the introductory part is not a complete sentence:

   > ✓ The winners are: Anna Singh
   >   Dieter Goering
   >   George Turner
   >   Hugh Mackay

2. **Use a colon for formality before a direct quotation or when a complete sentence precedes the quotation:**

   > The leaders of the anti-homework group repeated their message: "Children need less homework and more free time."

3. **Use a colon between numbers expressing time and ratios:**

> 4:30 p.m.

> The ratio of calcium to potassium should be 7:1.

Comma [,]

A comma indicates a brief pause in a sentence. It is the trickiest of all punctuation marks; even the experts differ on when to use them. Most agree, however, that too many commas are as bad as too few because they make writing choppy and awkward to read. Certainly contemporary writers use fewer commas than earlier stylists did. Whenever you are in doubt about using a comma, let clarity be your guide.

The most widely accepted conventions regarding the comma are as follows:

1. **Use a comma to separate two independent clauses joined by a coordinating conjunction (*and, but, for, or, nor, yet, so, whereas*).** By signalling that there are two clauses, the comma will prevent the reader from thinking that the beginning of the second clause is the end of the first:

> ✗ He went out for dinner with his sister and his roommate joined them later.

> ✓ He went out for dinner with his sister, and his roommate joined them later.

When the second clause has the same subject as the first, you have the option of omitting both the second subject and the comma:

> ✓ She can stickhandle well, but she can't shoot.

> ✓ She can stickhandle well but can't shoot.

If you mistakenly punctuate two sentences as if they were one, the result will be a *run-on sentence*; if you use a comma but forget the coordinating conjunction, the result will be a *comma splice* (see Chapter 14):

> ✗ We took the third graders to the zoo, it was closed for repairs.

> ✓ We took the third graders to the zoo, but it was closed for repairs.

Remember that words such as *however, therefore,* and *thus* are conjunctive adverbs, not conjunctions; if you use one of them to join two independent clauses, the result will again be a comma splice:

> ✗ She was accepted into teachers college, however, she took a year off to earn her tuition.

> ✓ She was accepted into teachers college; however, she took a year off to earn her tuition.

Conjunctive adverbs are often confused with conjunctions. You can distinguish between the two if you remember that a conjunctive adverb's position in a sentence can be changed:

> ✓ She was accepted into teachers college; she took a year off, however, to earn her tuition.

The position of a conjunction, on the other hand, is invariable; it must be placed between the two clauses:

> ✓ She was accepted into teachers college, but she took a year off to earn her tuition.

A good rule of thumb, then, is to *use a comma when the linking word can't move.*

When, in rare cases, the independent clauses are short and closely related, they may be joined by a comma alone:

> ✓ I came, I saw, I conquered.

2. **Use a comma between items in a series.** Place a coordinating conjunction before the last item:

> ✓ She finally found an apartment that was large, bright, and clean.

> ✓ Then she had to scrounge around for dishes, pots, cutlery, and a kettle.

The comma before the conjunction (known as a serial or Oxford comma) is optional for single items in a series:

> ✓ She kept a cat, a dog and a budgie.

For phrases in a series, however, use a serial comma to help to prevent confusion:

✗ When we set off on our trip, we were warned about passport thieves, attacks on single women and lost children.

In this case, a comma would prevent the reader from thinking that attacks were made on lost children as well as single women:

✓ We were warned about passport thieves, attacks on single women, and lost children.

3. **Use a comma to separate adjectives preceding a noun when they modify the same element:**

✓ It was a rainy, windy night.

However, when the adjectives do not modify the same element, you should not use a comma:

✗ It was a pleasant, winter outing.

Here *winter* modifies *outing*, but *pleasant* modifies the whole phrase *winter outing*. A good way of deciding whether or not you need a comma is to see if you can reverse the order of the adjectives. If you can reverse them (*rainy, windy night* or *windy, rainy night*), use a comma; if you can't (*winter pleasant outing*), omit the comma:

✓ It was a pleasant winter outing.

4. **Use commas to set off an interruption (or parenthetical element):**

✓ The film, I hear, isn't nearly as good as the book.

✓ The TA, however, couldn't answer the question.

Remember to put commas on both sides of the interruption:

✗ The music, they say was adapted from a piece by Mozart.

✓ The music, they say, was adapted from a piece by Mozart.

5. **Use commas to set off words or phrases that provide additional but non-essential information:**

   ✓ Our class president, Sue Stephens, does her job well.

   ✓ The golden retriever, his closest companion, went with him everywhere.

In these examples, *Sue Stephens* and *his closest companion* are *appositives*: they give additional information about the nouns they refer to (*president* and *golden retriever*), but the sentences would make sense without them. Here's another example:

   ✓ My oldest friend, who lives in Halifax, was married last week.

The phrase *who lives in Halifax* is a *non-restrictive modifier* because it does not limit the meaning of the word it modifies (*friend*). Without that modifying clause the sentence would still specify who was married. Since the information the clause provides is not necessary to the meaning of the sentence, you must use commas on both sides to set it off.

In contrast, a *restrictive modifier* is one that provides essential information; it must not be set apart from the element it modifies, and commas should not be used:

   ✓ The man who came to dinner was my uncle.

Without the clause *who came to dinner*, the reader would not know which man was the uncle.

To avoid confusion, be sure to distinguish carefully between essential and additional information. The difference can be important:

   ✗ Students, who are unwilling to work, should not receive grants.

   (All students are unwilling to work and should not receive grants.)

   ✓ Students who are unwilling to work should not receive grants.

   (Only those who are unwilling to work should be denied grants.)

6. **Use a comma after an introductory phrase when omitting it would cause confusion:**

   ✗ On the balcony above the singers entertained the diners.

   ✓ On the balcony above, the singers entertained the diners.

✗   When he turned away the student had disappeared.

✓   When he turned away, the student had disappeared.

7. Use a comma to separate elements in dates and addresses:

February 2, 2011 (Commas are often omitted if the day comes first: 2 February 2011.)

117 Hudson Drive, Edmonton, Alberta

They lived in Dartmouth, Nova Scotia.

8. Use a comma before a quotation in a sentence:

He said, "Life is too short to worry."

"The children's safety," he warned, "is in your hands."

For more formality, or if the quotation is preceded by a complete sentence, you may use a colon (see page 162).

9. Use a comma with a name followed by a title:

David Gunn, Vice-Principal

Patrice Lareau, M.D.

10. Do not use a comma between a subject and its verb:

✗   Her favourite flavour of all, is vanilla.

✓   Her favourite flavour of all is vanilla.

11. Do not use a comma between a verb and its object:

✗   He immediately decided, what he must do.

✓   He immediately decided what he must do.

12. **Do not use a comma between a coordinating conjunction and the following clause:**

> ✗ Ellen got honours but, Daniel failed the course.

> ✓ Ellen got honours, but Daniel failed the course.

Dash [—]

A dash (also called an em dash because it's about the same width as a capital letter *m*) creates an abrupt pause, emphasizing and setting apart the words that follow it. Never use dashes as casual substitutes for other punctuation; overuse can detract from the calm, well-reasoned effect you want to create.

1. **Use a dash to stress a word or phrase:**

> The British—as a matter of honour—vowed to retake the islands.

> Mr. Ramirez was well received in the school council—at first.

2. **Use a dash in interrupted or unfinished dialogue:**

> "But I thought—" Donald tried to explain, but Mario cut him off: "You were wrong."

The en dash (–) is shorter than an em dash and slightly longer than a hyphen, approximately the width of a capital letter *n*. It denotes that there is a range from one thing to another.

Use an en dash rather than a hyphen to separate parts of inclusive numbers or dates:

> The years 1890–1914

> pages 3–10

Ellipsis [. . .]

1. **Use an ellipsis (three periods) to show an omission from a quotation:**

For an ellipsis within a sentence, use three periods with a space before each and a space after the last:

> "The committee reported that medical tests . . . verified that alcohol was a factor in the fatal accident."

If the omission comes at the beginning of the quotation, an ellipsis is not necessarily used:

> The defence lawyer cited evidence that "verified that alcohol was a factor in the accident."

When the omission comes at the end of a sentence, use four periods with no space before the first or after the last:

> The judge noted that "alcohol was a factor. . . ."

To omit a full line of a poem, use a full line of periods:

> Cedar and jagged fir
>
> . . . .
>
> against the gray
>
> and cloud-piled sky

2. **Use an ellipsis to show that a series of numbers continues indefinitely:**

> 1, 3, 5, 7, 9 . . .

Exclamation Mark [!]

An exclamation mark helps to show emotion or feeling. It is usually found in dialogue and informal writing.

> "Woe is me!" she cried.

In academic writing, you should use it only in those very rare cases when you want to give a point emotional emphasis:

> The principal predicted that there would be no student failures this year. Some forecast!

Hyphen [-]

1. **Use a hyphen if you must divide a word at the end of a line.** Although it's generally best to start a new line if a word is too long, there are instances—for example, when you're formatting text in narrow columns

—when hyphenation might be preferred. The hyphenation feature in current word-processing programs has taken the guesswork out of dividing words at the end of the line, but in the event that you use manual hyphenation, here are a few guidelines:

a) Divide between syllables.

   con-join; mis-hap

b) Never divide a one-syllable word.

c) Never leave one letter by itself.

d) Divide between double consonants, unless they appear before a suffix. This exception does not apply if the second consonant has been added to use the suffix.

   ar-range; pass-able; begin-ning

2. **Use a hyphen to separate the parts of certain compound words:**

a) compound nouns:

   sister-in-law; vice-principal

b) compound verbs:

   test-market; dive-bomb

c) compound modifiers:

   a well-considered plan; forward-looking attitudes

Note that compound modifiers are hyphenated only when they precede the part modified; otherwise, omit the hyphen:

The plan was well considered.

His attitudes are forward looking.

Also, do not hyphenate a compound modifier that includes an adverb ending in *-ly*:

✗ a beautifully-written novel

✓ a beautifully written novel

Spell-checking features will help you determine which compounds to hyphenate, but there is no clear consensus, even from one dictionary to another. As always, consistency in your writing style is most important.

3. **Use a hyphen with certain prefixes (*all-*, *self-*, *ex-*) and with prefixes preceding a proper name. Again, practices vary, so when in doubt consult a dictionary.**

   all-star; self-imposed; ex-jockey; pro-Canadian

4. **Use a hyphen to emphasize contrasting prefixes:**

   The coach agreed to give both pre- and post-game interviews.

5. **Use a hyphen to separate written-out compound numbers from 1 to 99 and compound fractions:**

   eighty-one years ago; seven-tenths full; two-thirds of a cup

Parentheses [( )]

1. **Use parentheses to enclose an explanation, example, or qualification.**

   Parentheses show that the enclosed material is of incidental importance to the main idea of the sentence. They make an interruption that is more subtle than one marked off by dashes but more pronounced than one set off by commas:

   My wife (the eldest of five children) is a superb cook and carpenter.

   His latest plan (according to neighbours) is to dam the creek.

Remember that punctuation should not precede parentheses but may follow them if required by the sense of the sentence:

I like coffee in the morning (if it's not instant), but she prefers tea.

If the parenthetical statement comes between two complete sentences, it should be punctuated as a sentence, with the appropriate mark placed inside the closing parenthesis.

I finished my essay on April 30. (It was on Aristotle's ethics.) Then I had three weeks to study for the exam.

2. **Use parentheses to include additional details.** Information such as the date of a historical event or the abbreviation of an organization's name is placed within parentheses.

The Battle of Waterloo (June 18, 1815) marked the end of Napoleon's reign as emperor.

Juan was nervous about presenting at the Canadian Teachers' Federation (CTF) conference.

Like brackets, parentheses should not be overused.

Period [.]

1. **Use a period at the end of a sentence.** A period indicates a full stop, not just a pause.

2. **Use a period with some abbreviations.** It is still common, although not mandatory, to use periods in abbreviated titles (Ms., Dr., Rev., etc.), academic degrees (B.Ed., M.S.W., Ed.D., Ph.D., etc.), and expressions of time (6:30 p.m.).

However, Canada's adoption of the metric system in 1970 contributed to a trend away from the use of periods in many abbreviations. Provincial and state abbreviations do not require periods (NT, PE, NY, DC). In addition, most abbreviations for organizations no longer use periods (NAFTA, NORAD, CIDA, CBC).

3. **Use a period at the end of an indirect question.** Do not use a question mark.

> ✗ He asked if I wanted a substitute?

> ✓ He asked if I wanted a substitute.

> ✗ I wonder where she went?

> ✓ I wonder where she went.

4. **Use a period for questions that are really polite orders:**

> Will you please send him the report by Friday.

Question Mark [?]

Sometimes more formally referred to as an interrogation point, a question mark always indicates a direct question.

> Where did you do your student teaching?

> Who is your ethics instructor?

> How old is your daughter?

Quotation Marks [" "] and [' ']

1. **Use quotation marks to signify direct discourse (the actual words of a speaker):**

> I asked, "What is the matter?"

> "I have a pain in my big toe," he replied.

2. **Use quotation marks to show that words themselves are the issue:**

> The tennis term "love" comes from the French word for "egg."

Alternatively, as is done in this book, you may italicize the terms in question.

Sometimes quotation marks are used to mark a slang word or inappropriate usage to show that the writer is aware of the difficulty:

> Several of the "experts" did not seem to know anything about the topic.

Use this device only when necessary. In general, it's better to let the context show your attitude or to choose another term.

3. **Use quotation marks to enclose the titles of poems, short stories, songs, and articles in books or journals.** In contrast, titles of books, paintings, films, or CDs are italicized:

> The story I like best in Robert Weaver's *Canadian Short Stories* is "Bernadette" by Mavis Gallant.

4. **Use single quotation marks to enclose quotations within quotations:**

> He said, "Several of the 'experts' did not know anything about the topic."

5. **Do not use quotation marks for indented block quotations.**
   Other punctuation marks are placed either inside or outside quotation marks. A comma or period always goes inside the quotation marks:

> He said, "I think we can finish it tonight," but I told him, "Conrad, it's time to go home."

A semicolon or colon always goes outside the quotation marks:

> Conrad calls it "a masterpiece"; I call it junk.

A question mark, dash, or exclamation mark goes inside the quotation marks only if it is part of the quotation:

> She asked, "What *is* that, Conrad?"
>
> Did she really call it "a piece of junk"?
>
> You could hardly call it "a masterpiece"!
>
> I was just telling Louisa, "I think it looks like—" when Conrad walked into the room.

When a reference is given at the end of a quotation, the quotation marks precede the parentheses and the sentence punctuation is at the end:

> Lipsey suggested that we should "abandon the Foreign Investment Review Agency" (Paisley, 2004).

Semicolon [;]

1. **Use a semicolon to join independent clauses (complete sentences) that are closely related:**

   > For five days he worked nonstop; by Saturday he was exhausted.

   > His lecture was confusing; no one could understand the terminology.

   A semicolon is especially useful when the second independent clause begins with a conjunctive adverb such as *however, moreover, consequently, nevertheless, in addition,* or *therefore* (usually followed by a comma):

   > He ate a whole box of doughnuts; consequently, he felt sick in class.

   It's usually acceptable to follow a semicolon with a coordinating conjunction if the second clause is complicated by other commas:

   > Zoltan, my cousin, is a keen jogger in all weather; but sometimes, especially in winter, I think it does him more harm than good.

2. **Use a semicolon to mark the divisions in a complicated series when individual items need commas.** Using a comma to mark the subdivisions and a semicolon to mark the main divisions will help to prevent mix-ups:

   > ✗ He invited Professor Ludvik, the vice-principal, Christine Li, and Dr. Hector Jimenez.

   Is the vice-principal Professor Ludvik, Christine Li, or a separate person?

   > ✓ He invited Professor Ludvik; the vice-principal, Christine Li; and Dr. Hector Jimenez.

   In a case such as this one, the elements separated by the semicolon need not be independent clauses.

Slash [/]

The traditional slash is also referred to by many other terms, such as the *forward slash* (to distinguish it from the backward slash used in Web addresses), *slant*, *stroke*, *solidus*, and *virgule*.

1. **Use a slash to indicate a relationship between two or more ideas or things:**

   The ethical notions of Dewey/Kant agree on many levels.

   This examination will be graded as pass/fail.

2. **Use a slash to mark the end of a poetic line written in sentence form:**

   In early May/Upon the sand/I saw a man

3. **Do not include a space before or after a slash.**

   ✗ The incident was one of he said / she said.

   ✓ The incident was one of he said/she said.

STYLE TREATMENTS

Features such as boldface and stylish fonts allow you to add creative visual elements to your writing. Unfortunately, too many of these enhancements annoy readers and may detract from your ideas. Therefore, great care must be exercised when using any the following formats.

Boldface

While boldface calls attention to a specific point, it can overpower other elements if used too often. Aside from exceptional circumstances, use boldface for only the headings and subheadings in your writing projects.

Boldface does have a place in creative writing, where certain words take on specific intonation for artistic effect. However, for the most part, the bold icon in your word-processing program is best left untouched.

Highlighting

Using different colours can serve a valuable purpose in your diagrams, maps, and other visual pieces. They can make illustrations more appealing and emphasize aspects that are most relevant to your topic. However, highlighting should be reserved for these elements. Don't use background colours or patterns to showcase words, sentences, or paragraphs.

Italics

Unlike the other features discussed in this section, italics must be used at certain times in your writing. It is important, then, to understand when it is appropriate to use this format. Italics are primarily used to

- indicate the titles of books, long poems that are complete books, plays, films, CDs, and long musical compositions (*Fifth Business* is one of my favourite novels.);
- emphasize an idea (All equipment must be washed *immediately*.);
- identify a word or phrase that is the subject of discussion (The term *peer group* is used in sociology.); and
- indicate a foreign word or expression that has not been naturalized in English (The government was overthrown in a *coup d'état*.).

Font Changes

There are hundreds of fonts and sizes available in most word-processing programs. While there is still much discussion on this issue, the emerging standard for academic and research papers (and the one recommended in this book) is Times New Roman, size 12. This font is sometimes expressed as TNR12.

Except for the use of italics, keep to the same font and size throughout a piece of writing. There is rarely a need to mix different formats, and doing so may make your writing difficult to read. Further, the more complicated and cumbersome you make an essay, report, or paper, the greater the chance of errors and confusion.

Underlining

In the past, particularly when handwriting was the norm, underlining was used instead of italics. However, it is a technique that is now best avoided.

CHAPTER 16

Misused Words and Phrases

OBJECTIVES

- To highlight word confusions
- To target commonly misused words and phrases
- To illustrate proper usage

INTRODUCTION

Although we all have specific words and phrases that we have trouble using correctly, all educators need to be vigilant. Regardless of what grade or subjects you teach or the types of projects you assign, you must view the details and conventions of the English language carefully and seriously. Not only must you be an example of linguistic standards, but you must also always demand the same from your students.

This chapter lists some of the more common errors that continually appear in both written and spoken English. Electronic spell- and grammar checks will also help you avoid such errors. However, these programs are not foolproof. When in doubt, consult a dictionary, usage guide, or reputable website.

accept, except. Accept is a verb meaning to *receive affirmatively*; **except**, when used as a verb, means to *exclude*:

> I <u>accept</u> your offer.

> The teacher <u>excepted</u> him from the general punishment.

accompanied by, accompanied with. Use **accompanied by** for people; use **accompanied with** for objects:

He was <u>accompanied by</u> his wife.

The brochure arrived, <u>accompanied with</u> a discount coupon.

adage. An **adage** is a saying or short statement that has gained meaning over time. Therefore, you don't need to qualify it with the word *old*.

advice, advise. Advice is a noun, **advise** a verb:

He was <u>advised</u> to ignore the <u>advice</u> of others.

affect, effect. Affect is a verb meaning to *influence*; however, it also has a specialized meaning in psychology, referring to a person's emotional state. **Effect** can be either a noun meaning *result* or a verb meaning to *bring about*:

The eye drops <u>affect</u> his vision.

Because he was so depressed, he showed no <u>affect</u> when he heard the joke.

The <u>effect</u> of higher government spending is higher inflation.

She failed to <u>effect</u> more student participation in her classes.

all ready, already. To be **all ready** is simply to be ready for something; **already** means *beforehand* or *earlier*:

The students were <u>all ready</u> for the lecture to begin.

The professor had <u>already</u> left her office by the time Blair arrived.

all right. All right has become a catch-all phrase that borders on slang. Use it sparingly and always write it as two words: *all right*. This expression can mean *safe and sound, in good condition*, or *okay*; *correct*; *satisfactory*; or *I agree*:

Are you <u>all right</u>?

The student's answers were <u>all right</u>.

(Note the ambiguity of the second example: does it mean that the answers were all correct or simply satisfactory? In this case, it might be better to use a clearer word.)

all together, altogether. All together means *in a group*; **altogether** is an adverb meaning *entirely*:

> He was altogether certain that the children were all together.

allusion, illusion. An **allusion** is an indirect reference to something; an **illusion** is a false perception:

> The rock image is an allusion to the myth of Sisyphus.

> He thought he saw a sea monster, but it was an illusion.

a lot. Avoid using **a lot** in your professional and academic writing. If you do use this informal term, write it as two words: *a lot.*

alternate, alternative. Alternate means *every other* or *every second* thing in a series; **alternative** refers to a *choice* between options:

> The two sections of the class attended discussion groups on alternate days.

> The students could do an extra paper as an alternative to writing the exam.

among, between. Use **among** for three or more persons or objects, **between** for two:

> Between you and me, there's trouble among the team members.

amount, number. Amount indicates quantity when units are not discrete and not absolute; **number** indicates quantity when units are discrete and absolute:

> A large amount of timber.

> A large number of students.

See also **less, fewer.**

analysis. The plural is *analyses.*

anyone, any one. Any one is written as two words to give numerical emphasis; otherwise, it is written as one word:

> Any one of us could do that.

> Anyone could do that.

anyways. Non-standard. Use *anyway*.

as, because. As is a weaker conjunction than **because** and may be confused with *when*:

    ✗   <u>As</u> I was working, I ate at my desk.

    ✓   <u>Because</u> I was working, I ate at my desk.

as to. A common feature of bureaucratese. Replace it with a single-word preposition such as *about* or *on*:

    ✗   They were concerned <u>as to</u> the range of disagreement.

    ✓   They were concerned <u>about</u> the range of disagreement.

    ✗   They recorded his comments <u>as to</u> the treaty.

    ✓   They recorded his comments <u>on</u> the treaty.

bad, badly. Bad is an adjective meaning *not good*:

    The meat tastes <u>bad</u>.

    He felt <u>bad</u> about forgetting the dinner party.

Badly is an adverb meaning *not well*; when used with the verbs *want* or *need*, it means *very much*:

    She thought he played the villain's part <u>badly</u>.

    I <u>badly</u> need a new suit.

beside, besides. Beside is a preposition meaning *next to*:

    She worked <u>beside</u> her assistant.

Besides has two uses. As a preposition it means *in addition to*; as a conjunctive adverb it means *moreover*:

    <u>Besides</u> recommending the changes, the consultants are implementing them.

    It was time for lunch; <u>besides</u>, it was hot and we wanted to rest.

bring, take. One **brings** something to a closer place and **takes** it to a farther one:

> Next time you come to visit, <u>bring</u> your friend along.

> <u>Take</u> your umbrella with you when you go.

can, may. Can means to *be able*; **may** means to *have permission*:

> <u>Can</u> you fix the lock?

> <u>May</u> I have another piece of cake?

In everyday speech, **can** has evolved such that it covers both meanings; in formal writing and academic presentations, however, you must observe the linguistic distinction.

can't hardly. A faulty combination of *can't* and *can hardly* that is to be avoided. Use one or the other:

> He <u>can't</u> swim.

> He <u>can hardly</u> swim.

cite, sight, site. To **cite** something (in an academic paper, for example) is to *quote* or *mention* it as an example or authority; **sight** can be used in many ways, all of which relate to the ability to *see*; **site** refers to a specific physical *location*:

> You need to <u>cite</u> that source in your essay.

> His <u>sight</u> was extremely limited.

> That <u>site</u> is perfect for a neighbourhood pub.

complement, compliment. The verb to **complement** means to *complete* or *enhance*; to **compliment** means to *praise*:

> Her ability to analyze data <u>complements</u> her excellent research skills.

> I <u>complimented</u> her on her outstanding report.

The same rule applies when these words are used as adjectives. The adjective *complimentary* can also mean *free*:

Use complementary colours for that design.

That was a complimentary comment.

These are complimentary tickets.

compose, comprise. Both words mean to *constitute* or *make up*, but **compose** is preferred. **Comprise** is correctly used to mean *include, consist of,* or *be composed of*. Using **comprise** in the passive ("is comprised of")—as you might be tempted to do in the second example—is usually frowned upon in formal writing:

These students will compose the group that will go overseas.

Each paragraph comprises an introduction, an argument, and a conclusion.

continual, continuous. **Continual** means *repeated over a period of time*; **continuous** means *constant* or *without interruption*:

The strikes caused continual delays in building the road.

Five days of continuous rain ruined our holiday.

could of. This construction is incorrect, as are **might of, should of,** and **would of**. Replace *of* with *have*:

✗ He could of done it.

✓ He could have done it.

✓ They might have been there.

✓ I should have known.

✓ We would have left earlier.

council, counsel. **Council** is a noun meaning an *advisory* or *deliberative assembly*. **Counsel** as a noun means *advice* or *lawyer*; as a verb it means to *give advice*.

The college council meets on Tuesday.

We respect her counsel, since she's seldom wrong.

As a camp counsellor, you may need to counsel parents as well as children.

criterion, criteria. A **criterion** is a standard for judging something. **Criteria** is the plural of **criterion** and thus requires a plural verb:

> The major criterion was excellence of design.

> These are my criteria for grading the reports.

data. The plural of *datum*. The set of information, usually in numerical form, that is used for analysis as the basis for a study. Because **data** often refers to a single mass entity, many writers accept its use with a singular verb and pronoun:

> These data were gathered in an unsystematic fashion.

> When the data is in we'll have a look at it.

deduce, deduct. To **deduce** something is to *work it out by reasoning*; to **deduct** means to *subtract* or *take away* from something. The noun form of both words is *deduction*.

> You could deduce from his statement that the plant was about to close.

> We will deduct income tax from your January pay.

defence, defense. Both spellings are correct: **defence** is standard in Britain and is somewhat more common than **defense** in Canada; the latter is standard in the United States.

delusion, illusion. A **delusion** is a belief or perception that is distorted; an **illusion** is a false belief:

> He had delusions of grandeur.

> The desert pool he thought he saw was an illusion.

dependent, dependant. **Dependent** is an adjective meaning *contingent on* or *subject to*; **dependant** is a noun.

> Suriya's graduation is dependent upon her passing algebra.

> She has four dependants.

device, devise. **Device** is a noun meaning *an object used for a specific purpose*. **Devise** is a verb meaning to *form* or *create*.

The SMART Board is becoming a popular <u>device</u> in teaching.

Harry struggled to <u>devise</u> a suitable lesson plan.

different from, different than. Use **different from** to compare two persons or things; use **different than** with a full clause:

You are <u>different from</u> me.

This city is <u>different than</u> it used to be.

diminish, minimize. To **diminish** means to *make* or *become smaller*; to **minimize** means to *reduce* something to the smallest possible amount or size.

His resolve to travel will <u>diminish</u> as he gets older.

The regulation will <u>minimize</u> the impact of higher prices.

disinterested, uninterested. **Disinterested** implies impartiality or neutrality; **uninterested** implies a lack of interest:

As a <u>disinterested</u> observer, he was in a good position to judge the issue fairly.

<u>Uninterested</u> in the proceedings, he yawned repeatedly.

due to. Although increasingly used to mean *because of*, **due** is an adjective and therefore needs to modify something:

✗   <u>Due to</u> his impatience, we lost the contract. [*Due* is dangling.]

✓   The loss was <u>due to</u> his impatience.

e.g., i.e. Derived from Latin, **e.g.** (*exampli gratia*) means *for example* or *as an example*; **i.e.** (*id est*) means *that is* or *that is to say*. The terms cannot be used interchangeably.

exceptional, exceptionable. **Exceptional** means *unusual* or *outstanding*, whereas **exceptionable** means *open to objection* and is generally used in negative contexts:

His accomplishments are <u>exceptional</u>.

He was ejected from the game because of his <u>exceptionable</u> behaviour.

farther, further. Farther refers to physical distance, **further** to extent:

> He paddled <u>farther</u> than his friends did.

> She explained the plan <u>further</u>.

focus. The plural of the noun may be either *focuses* (also spelled *focusses*) or *foci*.

good, well. Good is an adjective that modifies a noun; **well** is an adverb that modifies a verb.

> He is a <u>good</u> rugby player.

> The experiment went <u>well</u>.

hanged, hung. Hanged means *executed by hanging*. **Hung** means *suspended* or *clung to*:

> He was <u>hanged</u> at dawn for the murder.

> He <u>hung</u> the picture.

> She <u>hung</u> on to the boat when it capsized.

heredity, hereditary. Heredity is a noun; **hereditary** is an adjective. **Heredity** is the biological process whereby characteristics are passed from one generation to the next; **hereditary** describes those characteristics:

> <u>Heredity</u> is a factor in the incidence of this disease.

> Your asthma may be <u>hereditary</u>.

hopefully. Use **hopefully** as an adverb meaning *full of hope*:

> She scanned the horizon <u>hopefully</u>, looking for signs of the missing boat.

In formal writing, using **hopefully** to mean *I hope* is still frowned upon, although it is increasingly common; it's better to use *I hope*:

> ✗   <u>Hopefully</u> the experiment will go off without a hitch.

> ✓   <u>I hope</u> the experiment will go off without a hitch.

i.e. See **e.g.**

illusion. See **allusion** and **delusion**.

incite, insight. Incite is a verb meaning to *stir up*; **insight** is a noun meaning (often sudden) *understanding*.

> His intention was to <u>incite</u> an uprising.

> Her <u>insight</u> into the situation was remarkable.

infer, imply. To **infer** means to *deduce* or *conclude by reasoning*. It is often confused with **imply**, which means to *suggest* or *insinuate*.

> We can <u>infer</u> from the large population density that there is a high demand for services.

> The large population density <u>implies</u> that there is a high demand for services.

inflammable, flammable, non-flammable. Despite its *in-* prefix, **inflammable** is not the opposite of **flammable**: both words describe things that are *easily set on fire*. The opposite of **flammable** is **non-flammable**. To prevent any possibility of confusion, it's best to avoid **inflammable** altogether.

irregardless. Non-standard. Use *regardless*.

its, it's. Its is a form of possessive pronoun; **it's** is a contraction of *it is*. Many people mistakenly put an apostrophe in **its** to show possession or use *its'*, which is not a word.

> ✗ The cub wanted <u>it's</u> mother.

> ✓ The cub wanted <u>its</u> mother.

> ✓ <u>It's</u> time to leave.

less, fewer. Less refers to quantity, **fewer** to number.

> He should have used <u>less</u> garlic in the sauce.

> There were <u>fewer</u> people at the rally than we had expected.

lie, lay. To **lie** means to *assume a horizontal position*; to **lay** means to *put down*. The changes of tense often cause confusion:

Present	Past	Past participle	Present participle
lie	lay	lain	lying
lay	laid	laid	laying

✗   I was <u>laying</u> on the couch when he came in.

✓   I was <u>lying</u> on the couch when he came in.

✓   I <u>laid</u> the table for dinner.

✓   She needed to <u>lie</u> down for a minute.

✓   The crew was <u>laying</u> the carpet.

like, as. **Like** is a preposition, but it is often wrongly used as a conjunction. To join two independent clauses, use the conjunction **as**:

✗   I want to progress <u>like</u> you have this year.

✓   I want to progress <u>as</u> you have this year.

✓   Prof. Bain is <u>like</u> my old school principal.

might of. See **could of**.

mitigate, militate. To **mitigate** means to *reduce the severity* of something; to **militate** against something means to *oppose* it:

This income will <u>mitigate</u> my overdraft problems.

His credentials will <u>militate</u> against the resistance to his appointment.

myself, me. **Myself** is an intensifier of, not a substitute for, *I* or *me*:

✗   He gave it to John and <u>myself</u>.

✓   He gave it to John and <u>me</u>.

✗   Jane and <u>myself</u> are invited.

✓   Jane and <u>I</u> are invited.

✓   I hesitate to mention <u>myself</u> here.

nor, or. Use **nor** with **neither**; use **or** by itself or with **either**:

> He is <u>neither</u> overworked <u>nor</u> underfed.

> The plant is <u>either</u> diseased <u>or</u> dried out.

off of. Remove the unnecessary **of**:

> ✗ The fence kept the children <u>off of</u> the premises.

> ✓ The fence kept the children <u>off</u> the premises.

phenomenon. A singular noun: the plural is *phenomena*.

plaintiff, plaintive. A **plaintiff** is a person who brings a case against someone else in court; **plaintive** is an adjective meaning *sorrowful*.

populace, populous. **Populace** is a noun meaning the *people* of a place; **populous** is an adjective meaning *thickly inhabited*:

> The <u>populace</u> of Hilltop Village is not well educated.

> With so many people in such a small area, Hilltop Village is a <u>populous</u> place.

practice, practise. Both of these spellings have become acceptable for either the noun or the verb. Just be consistent in whatever form you choose.

precede, proceed. To **precede** is to *go before* (earlier) or *in front of others*; to **proceed** is to *go on* or *ahead*:

> The faculty will <u>precede</u> the students into the hall.

> The medal winners will <u>proceed</u> to the front of the hall.

prescribe, proscribe. These words are sometimes confused, although they have quite different meanings. **Prescribe** means to *advise the use of* or *impose authoritatively*. **Proscribe** means to *reject, denounce,* or *ban*:

> The professor <u>prescribed</u> the conditions under which the equipment could be used.

> The student government <u>proscribed</u> the publication of unsigned editorials in the newspaper.

principle, principal. Principle is a noun meaning a *general truth* or *law*; **principal** can be used as either a noun, referring to the *head of a school* or a *capital sum of money*, or an adjective meaning *chief*:

> His lack of principle is a major problem.

> Bev Dawson is the principal of Richmond Secondary School.

> The principal reason for refusing is our lack of funds.

rational, rationale. Rational is an adjective meaning *logical* or *able to reason*. **Rationale** is a noun meaning *explanation*:

> That was not a rational decision.

> The president sent around a memo explaining the rationale for her decision.

real, really. Real, an adjective, means *true* or *genuine*; **really**, an adverb, means *actually*, *truly*, *very*, or *extremely*:

> The nugget was real gold.

> The nugget was really valuable.

seasonable, seasonal. Seasonable means *usual* or *suitable for the season*; **seasonal** means *of*, *depending on*, or *varying with the season*:

> It's quite cool today, but we can expect the return of seasonable temperatures later this week.

> You must consider seasonal temperature changes when you pack for such a long trip.

should of. See **could of**.

stationary, stationery. Stationary means *standing still*; **stationery** refers to paper and other writing or office supplies.

their, there, they're. Their is the possessive form of the third person plural pronoun. **There** is usually an adverb, meaning *at that place* or *at that point*. **They're** is a contraction of *they are*.

> They parked their bikes by the fence.

> I'll meet you there at midnight.

> They're going to France for the summer.

then, than. Then refers to a subsequent event or action; **than** indicates a comparison.

> Peter ran off with the ball, and <u>then</u> Sam chased him.

> Mary is heavier <u>than</u> Janice.

threw, through. Threw is the past tense of the verb to *throw*; **through** is a preposition that means *moving from one side of something to the other*:

> Sam <u>threw</u> the flower pot <u>through</u> the store window.

to, too, two. To is used in a variety of ways, including to indicate movement to a location or in a certain direction, a range between two things, or a relationship between objects or people. **Too** indicates an excess of something or acts as a synonym for *also*. **Two** is the written form of the numeral 2.

> I gave the paper <u>to</u> Mary.

> We ran out of chairs because <u>too</u> many parents came to the meeting.

> She has <u>two</u> younger brothers.

tortuous, torturous. The adjective **tortuous** means *full of twists and turns* or *circuitous*. **Torturous**, derived from *torture*, means *involving torture* or *excruciating*:

> To avoid heavy traffic, they took a <u>tortuous</u> route home.

> The concert was a <u>torturous</u> experience for the audience.

translucent, transparent. A **translucent** substance permits light to pass through it, but not enough for a person to see through; a **transparent** substance permits light to pass unobstructed, so that objects can be seen clearly through it.

turbid, turgid. Turbid, with respect to a liquid or colour, means *muddy* or *not clear*; with respect to literary style, it means *confused*. **Turgid** means *swollen*, *inflated*, or *enlarged* or (again with reference to literary style) *pompous* or *bombastic*.

unique. This word, which means *of which there is only one* or *unequalled*, is both overused and misused. Since there are no degrees of comparison—one thing cannot be "more unique" than another—expressions such as *very unique* or *quite unique* are incorrect.

while. To avoid misreading, use **while** only when you mean *at the same time that*. Do not use **while** as a substitute for *although, whereas,* or *but*:

> ✗   While she's getting fair marks, she'd like to do better.

> ✗   I headed for home, while she decided to stay.

> ✓   He fell asleep while he was reading.

-wise. Never use **-wise** as a suffix to form new words when you mean *with regard to*:

> ✗   Sales-wise, the company did better last year.

> ✓   The company's sales increased last year.

would of. See **could of**.

your, you're. Your is a possessive adjective; **you're** is a contraction of *you are*:

> Be sure to take your passport with you.

> You're likely to miss your train.

Educational Challenges and Research Topics

The following list includes many of the large and evolving concerns in education today. Some of these issues clash with personal values, and others generate passionate debate. In some cases, practical solutions and accommodations will not be realized. Nonetheless, these challenges need to be pondered and discussed.

The text accompanying each issue is not designed to narrow the investigation or express a particular opinion but merely to spark debate and highlight a sample of opposing perspectives. As you delve into these areas, you will discover many other viewpoints and contributing factors.

These subjects lend themselves to both individual and group study; they can be explored through oral presentations, debates, essays, etc. They also allow people to become personally involved in the discussion. For example, those who attended private school or remember the joys of homework, the struggles of dealing with a foreign language, or the anguish of being teased will be able to share their experiences.

1. **Lack of male teachers.**
   a) The vast number of female teachers has "feminized" elementary and middle schools and their attendant curricula.
   b) As long as a teacher follows the authorized curriculum, his or her gender is irrelevant.

2. **Academics versus vocational training.**
   a) Subjects such as woodworking, shop, small engine repair, and drafting have been removed from the official curriculum. Even physical education has been turned into heath education. These changes preclude students from gaining more practical and/or physical forms of learning.

b) Schools must concentrate on the core areas of language(s), sciences, and mathematics in order to educate twenty-first-century students properly.

3. **Students with special needs.**
   a) Students with special needs, whether physical, mental, or emotional, demand too much time and money, to the detriment of their classmates.
   b) We live in an inclusive society that should treat all people equally.

4. **Talented/gifted students.**
   a) Our best, brightest, and most creative students are not being encouraged or challenged because schools are overrun with weak students.
   b) No one is academically gifted in every subject. Even the best student can be emotionally immature; therefore, it is best to treat all students equally and allow gifted students to be role models.

5. **Effects of home environment/parental attitudes on student learning.**
   a) There are limits to what teachers/schools can accomplish because the home situation has far more power and influence over students.
   b) Teachers are often the most consistent presence in a young person's life.

6. **Religious instruction in schools.**
   a) Schools should be neutral places that exclude religious dogma.
   b) Religion grounds ethical interpersonal actions and cannot be divorced from any learning situation.

7. **The Pygmalion effect.**
   a) Teacher expectations influence a student's performance and behaviour.
   b) A child is either a good or poor student, regardless of what his or her teacher expects.

8. **Bullying.**
   a) Being bullied is simply a part of growing up.
   b) Bullying is a serious issue that must not be tolerated in any form or situation.

9. **Ethnic/cultural diversity in the classroom.**
   a) Our schools should encourage and celebrate diversity.
   b) There are simply too many competing interests; schools should concentrate on the dominant culture.

10. **Academic failure.**
    a) Failure is a necessary part of life that teaches us to work harder.
    b) Students learn at different levels and in different ways. We cannot enforce arbitrary achievement levels.

11. **Overprotection.**
    a) Removing playground equipment and banning tag and other kinds of ball games are symptoms of adult overprotection run amok.
    b) As adults, we have a responsibility to make sure that all children are safe.

12. **Private schools versus public education.**
    a) Private schools are elitist and openly discriminate against people of certain cultures, classes, races, and religions.
    b) Public education caters to all abilities and allows students to experience a more diverse landscape.

13. **Sex education.**
    a) If the schools do not deal with the subject, no one will, leading to more incidents of teen pregnancies and the spread of sexually transmitted diseases.
    b) Teaching children about sex is a parental responsibility that is embedded within a moral/religious base. As such, it should not be taught in school.

14. **Evolution.**
    a) Evolution is a basic tenet that grounds scientific thought and development.
    b) Human development must be placed within a religious/cultural framework.

15. **Feelings.**
    a) Learning includes many ups and downs and bruised egos.
    b) Schools should be happy and risk-free environments.

16. **Parental rights.**
    a) Parents have the right to remove their children from any class whose content clashes with their personal beliefs.
    b) All students must follow a common curriculum and attend all classes.

17. **Corporate sponsors.**
    a) Because many of our schools are deteriorating, it is perfectly appropriate to allow corporate sponsors to rebuild and maintain them. After all, many sports and entertainment venues are funded by corporations.
    b) Corporate sponsorship could lead to schools pushing the company's products and values, which staff and parents might oppose.

18. **Student failure equals teacher failure.**
    a) Teachers must be held accountable for the academic achievement of their students.
    b) Children and adolescents are free individuals and have a responsibility to read and study on their own.

19. **Student failure equals parent failure.**
    a) If students arrive late, do not do their homework, and/or exhibit a poor attitude, it is their parents' fault.
    b) Teachers have to take care of what happens in school and cannot use what occurs elsewhere as an excuse to ignore professional responsibility.

20. **Student failure equals student failure.**
    a) Learning and achievement fundamentally rest with the individual. We do a lifelong disservice to students when we imply that anyone else is responsible for their failure.
    b) There are always outside considerations and contexts that affect the learning environment; therefore, the larger educational community must be held accountable for student failure.

21. **Homework.**
    a) Homework is primarily repetitive and/or never corrected by the teacher. It is a worthless task that prevents students from engaging in more meaningful after-school activities.

b) Homework reinforces school lessons, teaches responsibility, and allows parents to keep abreast of their children's learning.

22. **School uniforms/dress codes.**
    a) Uniforms and dress codes not only make clothing decisions easier, but they also make students feel that they belong.
    b) Students need to express themselves, and their clothes are one way to do so.

23. **Tragedies.**
    a) Schools must address real-life issues such as car crashes, illness, and death.
    b) The topics of death and destruction should not be brought into the classroom. Schools should offer a protected environment for learning.

24. **Multiple languages.**
    a) Children cannot learn another language until they fully understand their respective mother tongue. Introducing too much information too early leads to confusion.
    b) Children are like sponges—the more early exposure to different languages the better.

25. **Libraries.**
    a) Learning is now an electronic endeavour. Old-fashioned physical libraries are unnecessary, poorly organized, too expensive, and impede the learning process.
    b) Not all knowledge is available electronically. Libraries encourage sharing and collaboration and therefore must be protected and developed.

26. **Book banning.**
    a) Books that contain racist or profane language, scenes, or imagery must be removed from school libraries and classroom reading lists because they do not represent modern morality and might offend particular groups.
    b) Banning classics such as *The Adventures of Tom Sawyer*, *The Merchant of Venice*, *The Story of Ferdinand*, and *The Giver* deny students the opportunity to confront and engage all aspects of the human condition over time and in different contexts.

27. **Technology versus tradition.**
    a) Schools must embrace emerging technologies (laptops, SMART boards, Internet, clickers, etc.) and transform the classroom into an interactive electronic space that highlights co-operation and new learning paradigms.
    b) Learning demands a human element; all the technology in the world will not replace human encouragement and feedback. Technology is simply the latest fad whose benefits are overblown and suspect.

28. **Homeschooling versus public education.**
    a) Learning at home shields a child from disruptions, poor role models, and incompetent teachers with outdated attitudes and slanted texts.
    b) No parent can be expected to master all of today's complicated and interrelated academic domains. Students should not be isolated from the larger community of peers.

29. **Scientific language versus educational gibberish**
    a) Education will never evolve into a respectable profession until it creates a field-specific vocabulary. Too often, the profession uses commonplace words that do not have a precise meaning.
    b) Education does not need to hide behind a specific language that creates a barrier to understanding. Further, we need to rid the field of words that are hurtful to others.

30. **Provincial/national control versus local control.**
    a) As schools are supported by local taxpayers, parents must control the schools and their curricula. They know what is best for their children and are well placed to drive the orientation of their local schools. Without an overextended infrastructure, more money can be spent on the students.
    b) A school has to cater to everyone within a geographic area. There must be a uniform and standard system for teacher certification and curriculum standards. Only an education administration can maintain such a system.

31. **Twelve-month versus ten-month school year.**
    a) To make the most of our schools' facilities and to maximize student learning, we must move to year-round schooling. Emerging research, as well as long-standing anecdotal evidence, maintains that long summer breaks impede learning processes.

b) Students and their families need significant amounts of time for other activities, such as attending camp, working, or travelling, and the summer is the perfect time for these endeavours. Besides, teachers also need a break.

32. **Handwriting versus keyboarding.**
    a) The majority of projects, especially in middle and secondary school, are written on a computer. Therefore, handwriting should be removed from the classroom.
    b) Despite the use of electronic communication, we continue to use handwriting in our everyday lives. In fact, penmanship is needed more than ever because it truly connects the writer to the words.

33. **Teacher status.**
    a) Regardless of the language appropriated, teachers are not considered professional in the legal sense of the term. Unlike nurses, doctors, lawyers, engineers, accountants, etc., teachers are (at best) a semi-profession or a regulated craft.
    b) Teachers are simply not qualified to self-regulate or adhere to a self-imposed code of conduct. Parents must exercise overall authority.

34. **Violence towards teachers.**
    a) Aggression directed towards a teacher, whether by a colleague, parent, or student, cannot be tolerated.
    b) Learning is an emotional and passionate experience. Parents must be permitted to defend their offspring vigorously.

Glossary

abstract language. Language that deals with theoretical, intangible concepts or details: e.g., *justice*; *goodness*; *truth*. (Compare **concrete language**.)

academic critique. A piece of writing that summarizes another work and includes a response to the work's main ideas.

acronym. A pronounceable word made up of the first letters of the words in a phrase or name: e.g., *NATO* (from *North Atlantic Treaty Organization*). A group of initial letters that are pronounced separately is an initialism: e.g., *CBC*; *NHL*.

active listening. A specific and focused form of non-judgmental listening.

active voice. See **voice**.

adjectival phrase (or **adjectival clause**). A group of words modifying a noun or pronoun: e.g., the dog *that belongs to my brother*.

adjective. A word that modifies or describes a noun or pronoun: e.g., *red*; *beautiful*; *solemn*.

adverb. A word that modifies or qualifies a verb, adjective, or adverb, often answering a question such as *how? why? when?* or *where?*: e.g., *slowly*; *fortunately*; *early*; *abroad*. (See also **conjunctive adverb**.)

adverbial phrase (or **adverbial clause**). A group of words modifying a verb, adjective, or adverb: e.g., *The dog ran* *with great speed*.

aesthetic reading. Reading for pleasure and experience.

agreement. Consistency in tense, number, or person between related parts of a sentence: e.g., between subject and verb or between noun and related pronoun.

ambiguity. Vague or equivocal language; meaning that can be taken more than one way.

annotated bibliography. A list of works that includes a brief description of each entry. (See also **bibliography**.)

antecedent (or **referent**). The noun for which a following pronoun stands: e.g., *cats* in *Cats are happiest when* *they* *are sleeping*.

application form. A specific document generated by an organization for hiring purposes.

appositive. A word or phrase that identifies a preceding noun or pronoun: e.g., *Joan, my aunt, is sick.* The second phrase is said to be in apposition to the first.

Aristotelian argument. A primarily verbal method of argument developed in ancient Greece and advocated by Aristotle. This method aims to have one view take precedent over another.

article. See **definite article**, **indefinite article**.

assertion. A positive statement or claim: e.g., *The data are inconclusive.*

auxiliary verb. A verb used to form the tenses, moods, and voices of other verbs: e.g., *am* in *I am swimming.* The main auxiliary verbs in English are *be, do, have, can, could, may, might, must, shall, should,* and *will.*

bibliography. 1. A list of works used or referred to in writing an essay or report. 2. A reference book listing works available on a particular subject.

book report/review. A summary of another work or, in education, an activity. Depending on the type of review (informative, analytic, or literary), the piece may include an assessment of the work's ideas and presentation.

case. Any of the inflected forms of a pronoun (see **inflection**).
  Subjective case: *I, we, you, he, she, it, they*
  Objective case: *me, us, you, him, her, it, them*
  Possessive case: *my/mine, your/yours, our/ours, his, her/hers, its, their/theirs*

circumlocution. A roundabout or circuitous expression, often used in a deliberate attempt to be vague or evasive: e.g., *in a family way* for "pregnant"; *at this point in time* for "now."

clause. A group of words containing a subject and predicate. An independent clause can stand by itself as a complete sentence: e.g., *I bought a hamburger.* A subordinate (or dependent) clause cannot stand by itself but must be connected to another clause: e.g., *Because I was hungry, I bought a hamburger.*

cliché. A phrase or idea that has lost its impact through overuse and betrays a lack of original thought: e.g., *slept like a log; gave 110 per cent.*

collective noun. A noun that is singular in form but refers to a group: e.g., *family; team; jury.* It may take either a singular or plural verb, depending on whether it refers to individual members or to the group as a whole.

comma splice. See **run-on sentence**.

complement. A completing word or phrase that usually follows a linking verb to form a subjective complement: e.g., (1) *He is my father*; (2) *That cigar smells terrible*. If the complement is an adjective it is sometimes called a predicate adjective. An objective complement completes the direct object rather than the subject: e.g., *We found him honest and trustworthy*.

complex sentence. A sentence containing a dependent clause as well as an independent one: e.g., *I bought the ring, although it was expensive*.

compound sentence. A sentence containing two or more independent clauses: e.g., *I saw the accident and I reported it*. A sentence is called compound-complex if it contains a dependent clause as well as two independent ones: e.g., *When the fog lifted, I saw the accident and I reported it*.

conclusion. The part of an essay in which the findings are pulled together or the implications revealed so that the reader has a sense of closure or completion.

concrete language. Specific language that communicates particular details: e.g., *red corduroy dress*; *three long-stemmed roses*. (Compare **abstract language**.)

conjunction. An uninflected word used to link words, phrases, or clauses. A coordinating conjunction (e.g., *and, or, but, for, yet*) links two equal parts of a sentence. A subordinating conjunction, placed at the beginning of a subordinate clause, shows the logical dependence of that clause on another: e.g., (1) *Although I am poor, I am happy*; (2) *While others slept, he studied*. Correlative conjunctions are pairs of coordinating conjunctions (see **correlatives**).

conjunctive adverb. A type of adverb that shows the logical relation between the phrase or clause that it modifies and a preceding one: e.g., (1) *I sent the letter; it never arrived, however*. (2) *The battery died; therefore, the car wouldn't start*.

connotation. The range of ideas or meanings suggested by a certain word in addition to its literal meaning. Apparent synonyms, such as *poor* and *underprivileged*, may have different connotations. (Compare **denotation**.)

context. The text surrounding a particular passage that helps to establish its meaning.

contraction. A word formed by combining and shortening two words: e.g., *isn't* from *is not*; *we're* from *we are*.

coordinate construction. A grammatical construction that uses correlatives.

coordinating conjunction. See **conjunction**.

copula verb. See **linking verb**.

correlatives (or **coordinates**). Pairs of correlative conjunctions: e.g., *either/or*; *neither/nor*; *not only/but also*.

cover letter. A one-page formal letter that introduces other documents, particularly a CV or resumé.

curriculum vitae (CV). A formal summary of one's academic and work-related experiences. (Compare **resumé**.)

dangling modifier. A modifying word or phrase (often including a participle) that is not grammatically connected to any part of the sentence: e.g., *Walking to school, the street was slippery.*

definite article. The word *the*, which precedes a noun and implies that it has already been mentioned or is common knowledge. (Compare **indefinite article**.)

demonstrative pronoun. A pronoun that points out something: e.g., (1) *This* is his reason; (2) *That* looks like my lost earring. When used to modify a noun or pronoun, a demonstrative pronoun becomes a demonstrative adjective: e.g., *this* hat, *those* children.

denotation. The literal or dictionary meaning of a word. (Compare **connotation**.)

dependent clause. See **clause**.

diction. The choice of words with regard to their tone, degree of formality, or register. Formal diction is the language of orations and serious essays. The informal diction of everyday speech or conversational writing can, at its extreme, become slang.

direct discourse. See **discourse**.

direct object. See **object**.

discourse. Talk, either oral or written. Direct discourse (or direct speech) gives the actual words spoken or written: e.g., *Donne said, "No man is an island."* In writing, direct discourse is put in quotation marks. Indirect discourse (or indirect speech) gives the meaning of the speech rather than the actual words. In writing, indirect discourse is not put in quotation marks: e.g., *He said that no one exists in an island of isolation.*

education portfolio. A collection of papers, photos, awards, and other materials that document the significant aspects of an educator's schooling and/or experience.

efferent reading. Reading that aims to gain meaning and understanding.

ellipsis. Three spaced periods indicating an omission from a quoted passage. At the end of a sentence, use four periods.

essay. A literary composition on any subject. Some essays are descriptive or narrative, but in an academic setting most are expository (explanatory) or argumentative.

euphemism. A word or phrase used to avoid some other word or phrase that might be considered offensive or blunt: e.g., *pass away* for "die."

expletive. 1. A word or phrase used to fill out a sentence without adding to the sense: e.g., *To be sure*, *it's not an ideal situation.* 2. A swear word.

exploratory writing. The informal writing done to help generate ideas before formal planning begins.

formal letter. A type of communication that details a specific subject, such as a concern or action. Formal letters are printed on official letterhead.

fused sentence. See **run-on sentence**.

general language. Language that lacks specific details; abstract language.

gerund. A verbal (part-verb) that functions as a noun and is marked by an -ing ending: e.g., *Swimming can help you become fit.*

grammar. The study of the forms and relations of words and of the rules governing their use in speech and writing.

indefinite article. The word *a* or *an*, which introduces a noun and suggests that it is non-specific. (Compare **definite article**.)

independent clause. See **clause**.

indirect discourse (or **indirect speech**). See **discourse**.

indirect object. See **object**.

infinitive. A type of verbal not connected to any subject: e.g., *to ask*. The base infinitive omits the *to*: e.g., *ask*.

inflection. The change in the form of a word to indicate number, person, case, tense, or degree.

initialism. See **acronym**.

intensifier (or **qualifier**). A word that modifies and adds emphasis to another word or phrase: e.g., *very* tired; *quite* happy; *I* myself.

interjection. An abrupt remark or exclamation, usually accompanied by an exclamation mark: e.g., *Oh dear! Alas!*

interrogative sentence. A sentence that asks a question: e.g., *What is the time?*

intransitive verb. A verb that does not take a direct object: e.g., *fall*; *sleep*; *talk*. (Compare **transitive verb**.)

introduction. A section at the beginning of an essay that tells the reader what is going to be discussed and why.

italics. Slanting type used for emphasis or to indicate the title of a book, journal, long poem, play, film, CD, and long musical compositions.

jargon. Technical terms used unnecessarily or in inappropriate places: e.g., *peer-group interaction* for "friendship."

linking verb (or **copula verb**). A verb such as *be*, *seem*, or *feel*, used to join subject to complement: e.g., *The apples* were *ripe*.

literal meaning. The primary, or denotative, meaning of a word.

logical indicator. A word or phrase—usually a conjunction or conjunctive adverb—that shows the logical relation between sentences or clauses: e.g., *since*; *furthermore*; *therefore*.

misplaced modifier. A word or group of words that can cause confusion because it is not placed next to the element it should modify: e.g., *I* only *ate the pie*. [Revised: *I ate* only *the pie*.]

modifier. A word or group of words that describes or limits another element in the sentence: e.g., *The woman* with the black hat *donated a million dollars*.

mood. 1. As a grammatical term, the form that shows a verb's function.
Indicative mood: *She is going*.
Imperative mood: *Go!*

Interrogative mood: *Is she going?*
Subjunctive mood: *It is important that she go.*

2. When applied to literature generally, the atmosphere or tone created by the author.

narrative writing. In education, the writing of real experiences from one's work. These stories can be kept private (e.g., in a professional journal) or shared with others where appropriate.

non-restrictive modifier (or **non-restrictive element**). See **restrictive modifier**.

noun. An inflected part of speech marking a person, place, thing, idea, action, or feeling, and usually serving as subject, object, or complement. A common noun is a general term: e.g., *dog*; *paper*; *automobile*. A proper noun is a specific name: e.g., *Martin*; *Sudbury*.

object. 1. A noun or pronoun that completes the action of a verb is called a direct object: e.g., *He passed <u>the puck</u>*. An indirect object is the person or thing receiving the direct object: e.g., *He passed <u>Marcus</u>* (indirect object) *<u>the puck</u>* (direct object). 2. The noun or pronoun in a group of words beginning with a preposition: e.g., *at <u>the house</u>*; *about <u>her</u>*; *for <u>me</u>*.

objective complement. See **complement**.

objectivity. A position or stance taken without personal bias or prejudice. (Compare **subjectivity**.)

outline. With regard to an essay or report, a brief sketch of the main parts; a written plan.

paragraph. A unit of sentences arranged logically to explain or describe an idea, event, or object. The start of a paragraph is sometimes marked by indentation of the first line.

parallel wording. Wording in which a series of items has a similar grammatical form: e.g., *At her wedding my grandmother promised <u>to love</u>, <u>to honour</u>, and <u>to obey</u> her husband.*

paraphrase. Restate in different words.

parentheses. Curved lines enclosing and setting off a passage; not to be confused with brackets, which are square.

parenthetical element. A word or phrase inserted as an explanation or afterthought into a passage that is grammatically complete without it: e.g.,

My musical career, if it can be called that, consisted of playing the triangle in kindergarten.

participle. A verbal (part-verb) that functions as an adjective. Participles can be either present (e.g., *speaking to the assembly*) or past (e.g., *spoken before the jury*).

part of speech. Each of the major categories into which words are placed according to their grammatical function. Traditional grammar classifies words based on eight parts of speech: adjectives, adverbs, conjunctions, interjections, nouns, prepositions, pronouns, and verbs.

passive voice. See **voice**.

past participle. See **participle**.

periodic sentence. A sentence in which the normal order is inverted or in which an essential element is suspended until the very end: e.g., *Out of the house, past the grocery store, through the school yard, and down the railway tracks raced the frightened boy.*

person. In grammar, the three classes of personal pronouns referring to the person speaking (first person), the person spoken to (second person), and the person spoken about (third person). With verbs, only the third-person singular has a distinctive inflected form.

personal pronoun. See **pronoun**.

phrase. A unit of words lacking a subject–predicate combination, typically forming part of a clause. The most common kind is the prepositional phrase—a unit consisting of a preposition and an object: e.g., *They are waiting at the house.*

plural. Indicating two or more in number. Nouns, pronouns, and verbs all have plural forms.

possessive case. See **case**.

prefix. An element placed in front of the root form of a word to make a new word: e.g., *pro-*; *in-*; *sub-*; *anti-*. (Compare **suffix**.)

preposition. The introductory word in a unit of words containing an object, thus forming a prepositional phrase: e.g., *under the tree*, *before my time*.

present participle. See **participle**.

professional journal. An individual's regular written record of workplace activities and observations; can be a private or shared document.

pronoun. A word that stands in for a noun: e.g., *she*, *this*.

punctuation. A conventional system of signs (e.g., comma, period, semi-colon) used to indicate stops or divisions in a sentence and to make meaning clearer.

reference works. Sources consulted when preparing an essay or report.

referent. See **antecedent**.

reflexive verb. A verb that has an identical subject and object: e.g., *Isabel taught herself to skate.*

register. The degree of formality in word choice and sentence structure.

relative clause. A clause introduced by a relative pronoun: e.g., *The man who came to dinner is my uncle.*

relative pronoun. *Who*, *which*, *what*, *that*, or their compounds, used to introduce an adjective or noun clause: e.g., *the house that Jack built*; *whatever you say.*

report card. An official record of student achievement at a specific period in time.

restrictive modifier (or **restrictive element**). A phrase or clause that identifies or is essential to the meaning of a term: e.g., *The book that my aunt gave me is missing.* It should not be set off by commas. A non-restrictive modifier is not needed to identify the term and is usually set off by commas: e.g., *This book, which my aunt gave me, is one of my favourites.*

resumé. A two-page summary of one's curriculum vitae, targeted for a particular job. (Compare **curriculum vitae**.)

rhetorical question. A question asked and answered by a writer or speaker to draw attention to a point; no response is expected from the audience: e.g., *How significant are these findings? In my opinion, they are extremely significant, for the following reasons. . . .*

Rogerian method. Developed by Carl R. Rogers, a method of argumentation that is more empathetic and less confrontational than an Aristotelian argument.

run-on sentence. A sentence that continues beyond the point where it should have stopped. The term covers both the comma splice (two sentences incorrectly joined by a comma) and the fused sentence (two sentences incorrectly joined without any punctuation).

sentence. A grammatical unit that includes both a subject and a verb. The end of a sentence is marked by a period.

sentence fragment. A group of words lacking either a subject or a verb; an incomplete sentence.

simple sentence. A sentence made up of only one clause: e.g., *Joaquim climbed the tree.*

slang. Colloquial speech considered inappropriate for academic writing; it is often used in a special sense by a particular group: e.g., *dope* for "good" or *diss* for "disrespect."

split infinitive. A construction in which a word is placed between *to* and the base verb: e.g., *to completely finish.* Many still object to this kind of construction, but splitting infinitives is sometimes necessary when the alternatives are awkward or ambiguous.

squinting modifier. A kind of misplaced modifier that could be connected to elements on either side, making meaning ambiguous: e.g., *When he wrote the letter finally his boss thanked him.*

standard English. The English currently spoken or written by literate people and widely accepted as the correct and standard form.

subject. In grammar, the noun or noun equivalent with which the verb agrees and about which the rest of the clause is predicated: e.g., *They swim every day when the pool is open.*

subjective complement. See **complement**.

subjectivity. A stance that is based on personal feelings or opinions and is not impartial. (Compare **objectivity**.)

subjunctive. See **mood**.

subordinate clause. See **clause**.

subordinating conjunction. See **conjunction**.

subordination. Making one clause in a sentence dependent on another.

suffix. An element added to the end of a word to form a derivative: e.g., *prepare, preparation*; *sing, singing*. (Compare **prefix**.)

summary. A brief and impartial account of a publication's or event's main points.

synonym. A word with the same dictionary meaning as another word: e.g., *begin* and *commence*.

syntax. Sentence construction; the grammatical arrangement of words and phrases.

tense. A set of inflected forms taken by a verb to indicate the time (i.e., past, present, future) of the action.

theme. A recurring or dominant idea.

thesis statement. A one-sentence assertion that gives the central argument of an essay.

topic sentence. The sentence in a paragraph that expresses the main or controlling idea.

transactional theory. Developed by Louise M. Rosenblatt, the concept that reading creates a unique interaction between the reader and the text.

transition word. A word that shows the logical relation between sentences or parts of a sentence and thus helps to signal the change from one idea to another: e.g., *therefore*; *also*; *however*.

transitive verb. A verb that takes an object: e.g., *hit*; *bring*; *cover*. (Compare **intransitive verb**.)

usage. The way in which a word or phrase is normally and correctly used; accepted practice.

verb. That part of a predicate expressing an action, state of being, or condition that tells what a subject is or does. Verbs are inflected to show tense (time). The principal parts of a verb are the three basic forms from which all tenses are made: the base infinitive, the past tense, and the past participle.

verbal. A word that is similar in form to a verb but does not function as one: a participle, a gerund, or an infinitive.

voice. The form of a verb that shows whether the subject acted (active voice) or was acted upon (passive voice): e.g., He <u>stole</u> the money (active). *The money <u>was stolen</u> by him* (passive). Only transitive verbs (verbs taking objects) can be passive.

Index

NOTE: Some terms not listed here may be found in the glossary.

THE MAKING SENSE SERIES

Margot Northey with Joan McKibbin
MAKING SENSE
A Student's Guide to Research and Writing
Seventh Edition

Margot Northey, David B. Knight, and Dianne Draper
MAKING SENSE IN GEOGRAPHY AND ENVIRONMENTAL SCIENCES
A Student's Guide to Research and Writing
Fifth Edition

Margot Northey and Judi Jewinski
MAKING SENSE IN ENGINEERING AND THE TECHNICAL SCIENCES
A Student's Guide to Research and Writing
Fourth Edition

Margot Northey, Lorne Tepperman, and Patrizia Albanese
MAKING SENSE IN THE SOCIAL SCIENCES
A Student's Guide to Research and Writing
Fifth Edition

Margot Northey and Patrick von Aderkas
MAKING SENSE IN THE LIFE SCIENCES
A Student's Guide to Research and Writing

Margot Northey, Bradford A. Anderson, and Joel N. Lohr
MAKING SENSE IN RELIGIOUS STUDIES
A Student's Guide to Research and Writing

Margot Northey and Brian Timney
MAKING SENSE IN PSYCHOLOGY
A Student's Guide to Research and Writing

Margot Northey and Jon G. Bradley
MAKING SENSE IN EDUCATION
A Student's Guide to Research and Writing